Contents

Introduction

In this handbook I have tried to present the basic processes in pottery in a simple, concise way, yet with sufficient depth to show how they can be developed. Having taught pottery to children and adults, I know that when I first started teaching I would have welcomed some guide for reference. I hope anyone in a similar position will find this book useful. Any advice in the book is the result of my experience both as a teacher and a potter; while the book is primarily intended as a guide for teachers of pottery, I hope that it will also be of interest to students of the craft and to more experienced potters.

The increase in the number of studio potters and the introduction of pottery into schools has prompted many people to take an active interest in making pots of their own. For all students, whether at school or attending further education classes, the basic needs are the same: comprehensive and clear explanation of the materials and equipment required, of the processes involved and a guide where to begin. All the processes necessary for making pots are dealt with in this book in chronological order; first, the preparation of clay, then methods of hand-building pots, decoration, throwing pots, glazing and firing. The technical terms and materials in use are fully explained and listed in a glossary.

In the chapter on 'Pottery in school' I have tried to answer the question 'Why teach pottery in school?' and have made practical suggestions on the methods that can be used. In no way is the chapter revolutionary; it is based on the situation that exists in our schools and does not profess to offer new ways of teaching children.

Most of the techniques described are applicable to any type of pottery, but I have dealt specifically with earthenware pottery fired in an electric kiln, simple earthenware glazes and basic throwing techniques. Where a process is long and complex, it has been broken down into tabulated steps to make it easier to follow.

Diagrams have been incorporated into the text whenever they help to clarify an activity. Photographs have been used extensively throughout to relate the techniques described to the results which can be achieved. These illustrate the best work from the past and give some idea of how pottery has developed in different countries of the world. Children's work too has been included to give some notion of the variety of things they find interesting and the sort of standards they can achieve.

My aim in this handbook is to present the facts in an intelligible way; I hope that I have also conveyed the excitement and sheer enjoyment of practising pottery.

Emmanuel Cooper

Illustrations

Photographs

We are grateful to the following for permission to reproduce photographs

Drawings
by Peter Branfield

1 Clay and its preparation

Clay has been used by man throughout recorded history because it can be moulded, because it keeps its shape and, after being subjected to heat, cannot be dissolved in water.

It is important that any serious approach to a craft such as pottery should be based on a thorough knowledge of basic processes; in pottery some understanding of clay as a medium of expression in its own right is necessary.

In school if the first processes in clay preparation can be tackled in the first two or three weeks of the term, the foundations will have been laid for all future work. This early emphasis on processes will also stress the fact that pottery is an art form which must be based on a thorough knowledge of technique.

Origins of clay

Clay is made up of decomposed feldspathic rock, and is the result of millions of years of natural activity: wind, rain, ice and water have eroded the rock and the resulting particles have formed beds of clay, some of which is highly plastic and is called ball clay. The rest has little plasticity and usually has a purer composition and is called primary clay.

Types of clay

China clay (Kaolin) is white in colour, has a very pure form, and is a primary clay; it was deposited where it was formed. It is found on outcrops of feldspathic rocks in large deposits in Devon and Cornwall. It is normally washed from the ground and this separates the quartz and other impurities from the clay. The huge white mounds surrounding the mines are in fact mainly quartz. China clay does not have sufficient plasticity to allow it to be used as a pottery body on its own, but forms the basis of many bodies when mixed with other clays and is, in fact, the basis of porcelain. It is also an important ingredient of many glazes.

Ball clay can be almost any colour, depending on the impurities it possesses. When clay was mined by hand it was dug with pointed shovels which gave the clay the appearance of balls—hence the name. It is similar in composition to china clay, but it has a number of organic impurities which give it its plasticity. It is known as a secondary clay because it has been moved, either by water or ice, from the place of formation; this movement has caused further grinding of the particles and the impregnation of organic impurities, giving it colour. The colour burns out during firing to leave a pale, creamy-white body.

Red terra-cotta is a secondary clay which has been impregnated with red iron oxide. This does not burn out but it does lower the melting point of the body and causes it to vitrify around 1150°C.

Secondary clays are deposited all over the country and tests can be made of any local deposits from a depth of about four feet. Large deposits are found in Staffordshire and Devon and are dug commercially there.

Commercially prepared clay

Clay is usually commercially supplied in polythene bags or wrappings; the clay is in a plastic state and contains about 25 per cent water. It has been mixed and prepared by the firm to their own specifications and suitable firing temperatures are usually recommended, both for biscuit and glaze firings. These prepared bodies are usually very reliable, especially at earthenware temperature, which is the temperature with which we shall deal. Two types of clay are usually listed in the catalogues: red or terra-cotta, and a white body which is usually slightly smoother. Other bodies may be listed as having a percentage of added grog, and these are often extremely useful to the potter. (Grog is dealt with later in this chapter.) The red body is, on the whole, probably more useful in the classroom as it fires to a pleasant soft red colour and becomes hard and vitrified at a fairly low temperature. On the other hand, the lighter bodies take glaze well, which shows them off to their best advantage. If there is sufficient space available, a quantity of both types of clay is desirable.

Clay preparation

Clay ordered from a supplier is often a blend of various bodies and several additions. It is normally in an almost ideal state and only requires wedging and kneading. However, as the clay becomes used and returned to the bin, it does need much more careful preparation. The various processes are dealt with below.

Layering is the process of slicing clay with a wire cutter when it is too hard and needs softening down. Each slice is dipped in water and the whole is banged back together. This banging is called wedging.

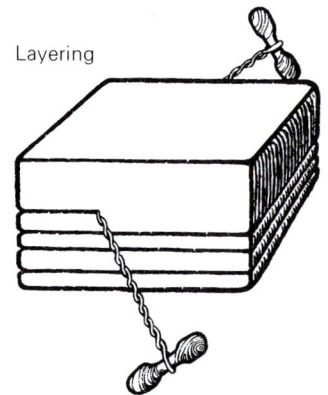

Layering

Wedging is the process by which hard and soft clay are mixed together. Clay taken from the bin is invariably in this hard and soft state.

Method

1. Knock the clay roughly into the shape of a brick and bang half of this on to the edge of the bench.
2. Use a wire to cut off the overhanging half; this should be banged on top of the clay left on the table.
3. Repeat this process until all moisture has been distributed throughout the clay, which should be a homogeneous mass.
4. At least ten bangs will be needed to accomplish this.

Some potters hold the view that, besides mixing the hard and soft clay together, the process forces the molecules of clay to move in the same direction and thus a stronger and more plastic body is formed. If done well, all air bubbles are removed and the clay is ready for use.

Incidentally, to prevent clay sticking to the table, it should be brought down at a slight angle to the surface.

Kneading is practised by the Japanese and is the process by which air is expelled from the clay, and the clay molecules are all moved in a similar direction, which gives it strength. There are two methods of kneading:

a. *Ox-head method.* The lump of clay is held firmly with the palms of both hands and is rocked in a clockwise direction upwards. The palms are now moved further round the clay, and the process repeated, so that the clay is moving round. The pressure exerted by the hands should be towards the centre of the clay and not directly downwards, or it will spread out into a sausage. Gradually a form resembling an ox-head will appear.

b. *The Oriental method* is probably more difficult to learn but more useful, as larger amounts of clay can be worked at the same time. The clay is

a–c Wedging

a

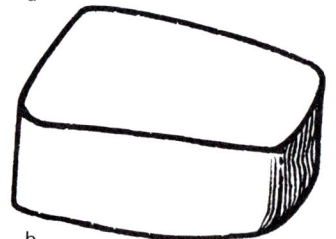

b

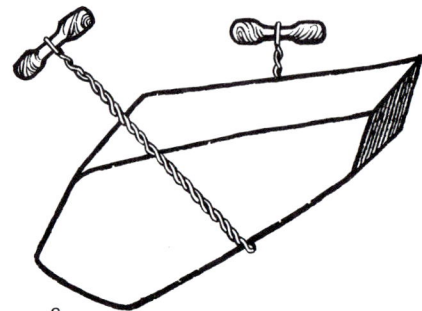

c

moved in two directions at once. The left hand moves the clay in a slightly vertical movement while the right hand moves it more horizontally. Both these movements are made at the same time and gradually the whole mass of clay should be moving. The form will be rather like a boxing glove.

In neither of these methods of kneading should clay be allowed to overlap and so trap in air. It is possible, when practising, to cut the clay to test for air bubbles, though experience will soon tell when the clay is ready for use.

Hardening or **drying** clay is necessary when it is too soft to hold its shape. Basically it has to be smeared on to an absorbent surface such as plaster or asbestos de-luxe. Plaster is perhaps the most useful and special blocks can be made to do the job if no table can be covered permanently with plaster. A covered table is not always successful as the surface gets damaged and needs renewing from time to time. The plaster also tends to take a long time to dry out and so looses its effectiveness. Blocks can be made using cardboard boxes as moulds which can easily be removed after the plaster has set. Three blocks, two-feet square, might prove to be more useful in a group rather than one large block, besides having the advantage of being relatively easy to move around.

Reclaim is clay which has been used and needs to be prepared for use again. There are usually two types:

a. Dried clay from work broken, or never finished or fired. This should be broken up and soaked in water until completely soft when surplus water can be poured away. This takes about two days. The soft clay can then be put out to dry on plaster, and wedged ready for use.

b. Soft, liquid slurry, normally from throwing on the wheel. This should be collected in a bucket and allowed to settle. Surplus water should be poured away and the process described above should be repeated.

Wedging benches must be solid and firm. Smooth wood is pleasant to work on and, being slightly absorbent, it prevents the clay from sticking. This is, however, a disadvantage when the clay does not require any drying. Formica surfaces are strong, tough and easy to clean and are very good. Zinc surfaced tables are not so pleasant but are very satisfactory. The wedging process itself should take place over a leg of the table, especially if the table is not too strong.

Slip is clay softened down in water and then put through a fine sieve to give it the smoothness of cream. This can be coloured by the addition of oxides. (See slips, later in this chapter.)

Additions to the body

Clay bodies can be made tougher or rougher by the addition of various ingredients.

1. *Grog* is fired clay which is ground down to various sizes and gives a body strength and texture. Being fired already, it cannot contract further and therefore lowers the amount the body can contract, which is very useful in large pots or models. It also helps to reduce warping and is an essential ingredient when making tiles. It can be quite rough on the hands when throwing, but it does add texture to the body. It is very useful for large coil pots. Up to 25 per cent can be added.

Drying

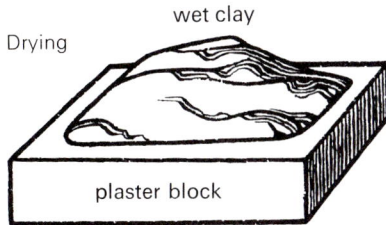

wet clay

plaster block

Kneading

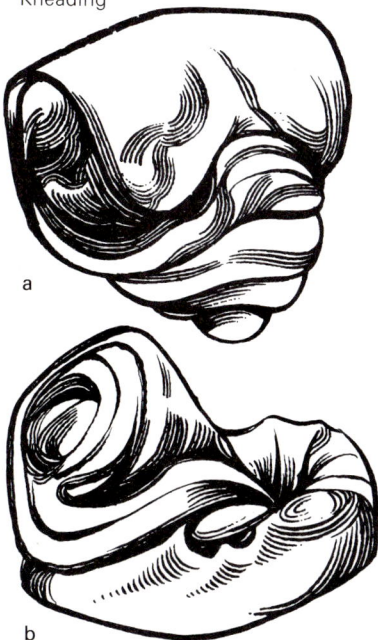

a

b

2. *Sand* makes a body stronger and more open for throwing. Up to 10 per cent can be added. It reduces the soapy quality some clays have.

Both these can be added to the clay while it is in its soft state. It is difficult to estimate exact quantities when water is present, but a rough measure could be 3 lb of grog to a bucketful of soft clay. A record can be kept, and if the recipe is satisfactory, it can be repeated. The whole bucketful can be stirred up and the grog or sand will in fact absorb quite a considerable amount of water and help to harden the mixture.

Other additions to the body are, on the whole, more complex.
Body stain is supplied by the manufacturers and can be added in the manner described above. Various oxides can also be added to colour the body, though the range is usually limited to darkening it. Experiments can be made with body stain and there seem to be many other possibilities, yet these have been unexplored until recently. Body stain was used extensively at one time for agate ware. Great restraint must be used if the results are not to be hard and crude. In school various methods of employing coloured clay can be very effective.

Clay chart

Clay has many physical states, each stage having its own possibilities and characteristics.

1. *As dug*   Lumpy non-homogeneous: generally containing a variety of foreign bodies such as vegetable matter or stones which render the clay unsuitable for use until it has been cleaned.

2. *Slurry*   Clay softened in water. Before being sieved it is lumpy and uneven. When sieved it is known as slip and can be used for joining leather-hard pieces of clay or for decoration.

3. *Plastic*   The water content is around 25 per cent and is suitable for throwing, modelling, etc. It does not feel sticky, nor does it crack if rolled into a coil and wrapped round a finger.

4. *Leather or cheese-hard*   Will bend, but only slightly. Ideal state for turning on the wheel, slab building, carving or incising and for slip decoration. Will support its own weight.

5. *Dry*   Very brittle and fragile state with no give. Tends to show lighter at the edges. If scratched the clay comes away as powder.

6. *Biscuit*   Once-fired clay and is now in a changed physical state. The body is strong, non-soluble and porous.

2 Decoration

It should go without saying that decoration must enhance the form of the pot and be a direct outcome of its shape. Plenty of reference should be made by the student to the pots decorated by earlier civilizations in which the form always predominated and not the decoration. The Bronze Age and Anglo-Saxon potters decorated their ware simply, with the most primitive of tools. The basic designs they used are the best examples of decoration at its most effective. (See Anglo-Saxon pot on p. 23.)

This chapter deals with the decoration of clay in its raw or green state. Underglaze painting is dealt with in the chapter on glazing.

1 Decorating with slip

Slip is a method of decoration using clays of different colour, and has its roots far back in English traditional work. It dates back to the time when little was known about glazes in England and the only glaze in common use was a transparent one with lead as its flux. The only way to introduce colour was with the use of coloured clays underneath this glaze.

In school, slip decoration has a directness which makes it understandable to most students. It requires some skill, but confidence and a clear idea of the pattern envisaged help to achieve reasonable results quickly. It is always useful to practise on the bench or on a discarded pot before the final piece is decorated, no matter what method of applying the slip is used, for at this stage it is boldness which is the main quality the student should be aiming at, and this can be encouraged if he knows exactly what the decoration is going to be.

Making slip

Sieving

Slips are made by putting softened clay through a sieve—usually 80 mesh. Red slip can be made by sieving the slurry collected from the wheel. A general rule in sieving is to use plenty of water, which helps the clay to go through easily and quickly. When the clay has settled, surplus water can either be poured or siphoned off. As a general guide, the slip should pour evenly and have the consistency of double cream. Naturally this means planning in advance when slip is required, as the clay takes some time to settle before water can be removed. The alternative, if the slip is required immediately, is to use the minimum amount of water, which makes the process slow and tedious.

Slip stains can be purchased from the manufacturers and a large variety of colours are available, though it is more interesting to use the basic oxides. The ready-made stains are often crude and have a commercial quality which is not always desirable in hand-made work. Cobalt, copper, manganese and iron oxides will give a variety of colours (see recipes).

There is little advantage in mixing small quantities of slip and a bucketful is a reasonable quantity which ensures a good supply, sufficient for the dipping of large pots.

Plastic buckets are quieter and easier on the hands than enamel ones and should have well-fitting lids. This prevents evaporation and protects the slip from foreign bodies. It should always be mixed thoroughly before use with either a paddle or, most effective of all, the arm. After the amount required has been removed, or the slip has been used, the walls of the bucket should be scraped with a rubber kidney or a sponge to remove any slip and thus prevent it drying and falling into the slip to make it lumpy. This may sound fussy but it does save time and effort and ensures the slip is always ready for use.

Slip is used as a simple method of decoration; it consists in covering the wall of the pot with a thin layer of a different coloured clay. There are variations on this technique and the slip can be applied in different ways which will be explained below, but the principle remains the same, and is probably the simplest way of adding colour and interest to a pot.

Slip trailers These are used to trail or pipe slip on to a pot or dish. There are two types of trailer:

a. The bulb type has many advantages and consists of a rigid rubber bulb and a nozzle. For use in the classroom it is invaluable. The trailer is simply filled by depressing the bulb and allowing it to fill itself through the nozzle. The only disadvantage is that the flow of slip is not always as even, nor is it obvious when the bulb is empty. Consequently air might be expelled, which can blotch a design.

b. The soft bag type which consists of a soft collapsible rubber bag and a nozzle. The trailer has to be filled through a funnel and little or no pressure has to be used to force the slip out. Its main advantage lies in the fact that the flow of slip is often very smooth and regular and it is obvious when the bag is nearly empty, and so the spluttering which can occur when air is expelled instead of slip can be avoided. The disadvantages are that it is tricky to fill and, once full, cannot be put on to the bench without slip running out.

Slip trailers should be washed out immediately after use as any slip which hardens is difficult to wash out, and the nozzle must be clean.

Slip trailers

Right: slip trailed decoration on a thrown and carved candlestick. Wrotham, Kent

Far right: slipware dish showing Charles II in an oak tree, surrounded by a lion and a unicorn. Seventeenth century English

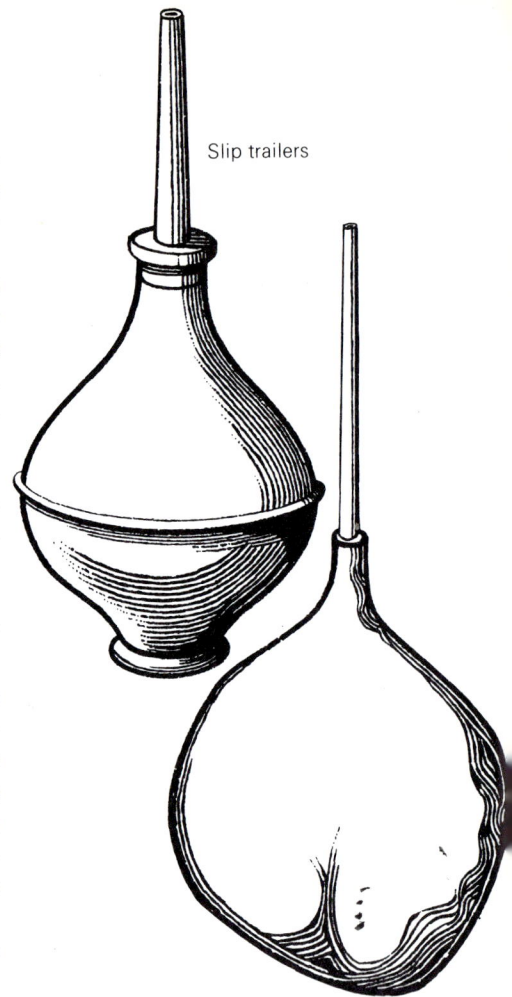

Feathering

Methods

Slip trailing. The slip should have the consistency of cream and should be very smooth and free from lumps, having been sieved at least twice through an 80 mesh sieve. Oxides should have been added before sieving to enable them to be well mixed.

The slip should be thoroughly stirred before use and all tools should be clean.

Trailing can be practised first of all either on the bench top or on old pots. It is easier to work standing and hold the trailer with both hands, arms tucked into the sides for support. The nozzle of the trailer should not actually touch the surface on which the slip is being trailed, but should be $\frac{1}{10}$" above it so that the slip is almost poured or dragged out. The movements should be as free and relaxed as possible and should be movements of the whole arm and not merely of the wrist. They should be confident and bold. Slip trailing has a fresh, bold, simple quality rather than a soft, subtle one, and this should be made evident both in the choice of design and in the execution of it.

Slip can be trailed either on to a layer of damp slip or directly on to the body itself. This is an effective method which causes the slip to remain raised on the surface.

Feathering is a method of decoration in which different coloured slips are laid alongside and drawn across each other with a fine point. It was usual to use a feather for this, hence the name. One method of working is to cover the inside of a low dish or slab of clay with a layer of slip; across this is trailed slip of a different colour. A fine strand of wire or a bristle from a brush is now drawn lightly across the slip to achieve the desired effect. (See diagram.)

Brushed slip. A brush can be used to apply slip, though it must be full and large, as slip must be applied thickly for several reasons:

1. Slip contains about 50 per cent water which, when it evaporates, leaves a very thin layer of clay.
2. A certain amount of clay always burns away in the firing and this must be compensated for when the slip is being applied.
3. Thin slip looks weak and mean.

Therefore:

1. Slip used for brush-work must be thicker than normal.
2. The brush should be reloaded after each brush stroke and as far as possible only single brush strokes should be made.
3. A bold, simple design suited to the method of decoration should be used, e.g. birds, animals, foliage.

Wax resist. This method of decoration is suitable both for slip and glaze decoration.

The wax is heated; ordinary paraffin wax candles plus a little turpentine or paraffin to thin it down is excellent, either in a water bath, which is safe but fails to get the wax as hot as is desirable, or over a candle or a low bunsen flame. This latter method can be dangerous as the wax can catch fire, and also, if the wax gets overheated, it evaporates in thick blue smoke which has a very unpleasant smell. I would recommend the water bath method for use in school.

The hot wax is now painted on to the clay body and when slip is

Flask with inlay of white slip. Sussex, nineteenth century

Pot with incised pattern and decorated with white slip. Wrotham, Kent, dated 1726

Dish with incised decoration of flowers and suns in dark brown and orange slip

Harvest jug with decoration scratched through white slip. Barnstaple, Devon, 1708

Water bath

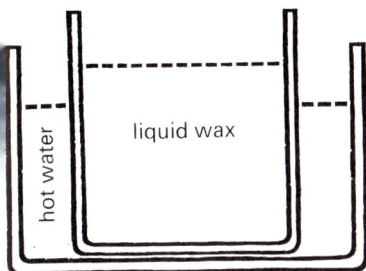

Vest African cooking pots with incised decoration

Part of a series of tiles showing imaginary scenes from the life of Christ, scratched through white slip

poured over the pot, the wax resists the slip which flows off. Liquid wax polish, which melts more easily in a water bath, can be used instead of the candles, though it is much more expensive.

A commercial water-based emulsion is now available which is much more convenient. In quantity it is water solvent and only becomes water resistant after being brushed on to the pot and allowed to dry. If the brush is washed in water immediately after use then it is unharmed. On the whole it is more convenient than wax.

Slip can only be put on most pots when the clay is leather-hard. It should only be put on one side at a time, and then allowed to become leather-hard before the other side is covered. When a pot or bowl is to be covered with slip both inside and out, the inside is covered first.

Slip is a quick and exciting method of decoration. It has many possibilities and is relatively uncomplicated and straightforward. It can be used on most types of pots and different methods for its use can be combined together. Other uses for slip will be dealt with later in the book.

2 Incised decoration

Incised decoration cuts into the surface of the pot. Tools can either be pressed into the surface of the clay or clay can be cut or gouged away. Early English and Roman pots have beautiful examples of this type of decoration. The patterns were simple and well suited to the medium of clay.

Before actually beginning to decorate a pot, it is often useful to establish exactly what a pattern is. Most children have only the vaguest idea of what a pattern can be and I have found it useful to make sure first of all that everyone is talking about the same thing. It seems to me that, simply, a pattern is a motif which repeats itself in some sort of order; a design, on the other hand, is an arrangement of shapes which is both pleasing and dynamic but is not necessarily a pattern.

One must also consider the shapes made by the spaces in between the actual impressions of the tool. These are as important as the tool marks themselves.

Gouged and carved patterns can range in scale from huge architectural pieces to small textured squares decorated with a scraper board nib, and tools used must be related both to the amount of space to be decorated and to the size of the pot.

The principles of pattern-making apply to all methods of decoration. *Rollers* are simple tools for applying incised decoration to a pot. They have been used for centuries to obtain quick, simple but effective patterns on pots, and they have the advantage of speed in producing repeating patterns. They can be made simply either of wood or of plaster. The surface needs to be carved in a simple, direct way and a piece of wire can be fitted for a handle. This can be rolled round the pot either on the rim, a favourite choice of the early potters in this country, or on a strong shoulder of the pot.

3 Sgraffito decoration

Sgraffito in its simplest form is merely scratching on clay. This can be made more effective by first covering the area with a layer of slip, allowing it to get leather-hard, and then either scratching or carving through this layer to reveal the clay underneath. The scratching can produce a textured, highly decorative design, while the cuts have a pleasant, clean, crisp quality. Lino cutting tools are excellent for carving into leather-hard clay.

The reverse process can also be used most effectively. A sharp-edged tool can be pressed cleanly into the clay surface, which may have to be slightly softer than usual, and the impression filled with slip of different colour. Several layers may be required, with drying intervals in between, before the slip has been built up above the surface and remains there when leather-hard. This surface slip can be gently scraped down until only the impression is full of slip. Type is excellent for this process and though the effect is slightly mechanical, interesting patterns can be built up.

This process is developed from the medieval technique of encaustic tile-making. (See Chapter 3, Tiles.)

4 Relief decoration

Relief decoration is made when clay is added instead of being taken away, and the surface is built up. The simplest method is to press strips or balls of clay, which could be a contrasting colour, on to the surface of the pot. These can either be left or can be decorated with incised patterns, and a rich effect can be achieved. Although it is often difficult to fix different clays together, it can be done by using a slip of equal proportions of both clays.

There is also another point to be watched: the pot must not be too hard, nor must the clay being added be too soft or, as the decoration dries and contracts, it may be split or even pull away from the surface. Little trouble will be experienced if the following points are watched as carefully as possible.

1. Both clays should be, as far as possible, in the same state of softness.
2. Both surfaces should be scored so that they are able to get a good bite into each other.
3. Slip or slurry should be painted on to the surfaces to help them to join together.
4. The two surfaces should be pressed as firmly together as possible.
5. When two different clays are being joined together, the slip should consist of equal proportions of each clay.

5 Sprigging

Sprigging is a more advanced form of relief decoration and consists of finely modelled clay motifs, made in a mould, being joined on to the side of pots. It was developed by the salt-glaze potters who found that fine details of modelling were accentuated by the fine, thin glaze that salt gave. Josiah Wedgwood also developed the technique of sprigging on his famous Jasper ware. On to a coloured clay body he joined finely modelled sprigging in a white clay in imitation of the Portland vase. This technique proved to be very popular and the skill required and the fineness of the modelling can be greatly admired today. These fine sprigs were made first of all by being modelled several times larger than the final result. This allowed the inclusion of very fine detail. A cast was

Carved wooden roller for decorating pots. Abuja, Nigeria

Tiles with relief decoration. Early English

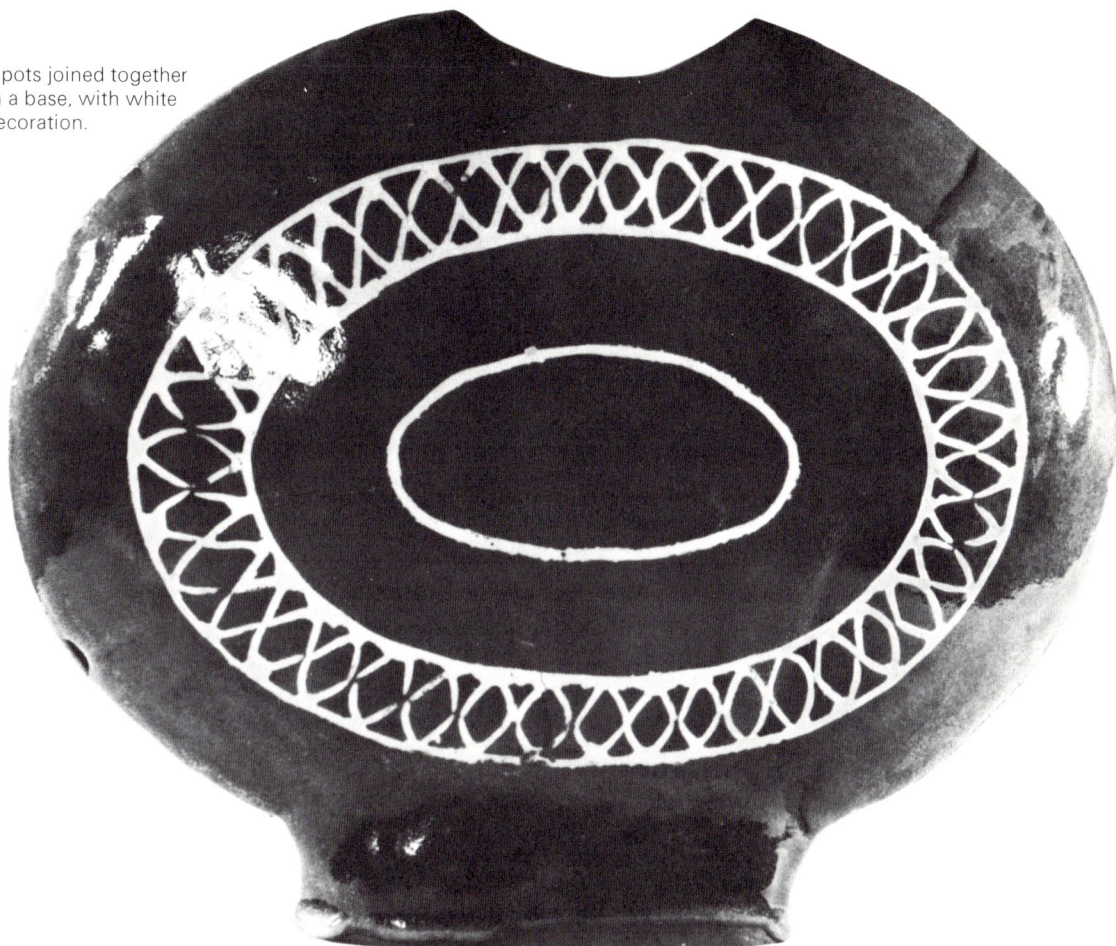

Two mould pots joined together mounted on a base, with white slip inlaid decoration.
Child 16

Teapot with applied moulded decoration. Salt glazed. English 1730

Thrown punch bowl, with applied moulded white clay, showing the scene of a sea battle. English, dated 22 November 1739

taken and an impression, in clay, taken of it. This was fired and of course contracted; the processes were repeated until the mould was the required size.

The method of making sprigs today is very similar:

1. The original is made—make sure that there is no undercutting which would prevent the cast coming out.
2. A plaster cast of this is taken and the original removed from it. Ensure that the cast is clean, if necessary, it can be washed gently with water.
3. Further definition can be scratched into the plaster if necessary.
4. To make the sprigs, soft clay should be used and pressed firmly into the mould; any protruding surplus clay should be removed and the surface made as flat and even as possible.
5. The sprig can be pulled from the mould with a ball of clay, or it can be pushed directly on to the pot if the surface allows this. Sprigs taken out can be allowed to dry slightly before being put on to the pot.
6. As plaster is absorbent, little difficulty will be experienced in getting the sprigs out.
7. The sprigs should be joined on to the pot as any other two clays are joined together.
8. The design can be carved directly into the plaster for a sharper effect.

Tools

Tools can be an interesting source of inspiration for decoration and need to be cared for and collected. Pottery modelling tools are carved out of box wood which has a fine grain which helps to prevent the wood from splitting and makes fine edges possible. These tools are expensive and if misused they quickly lose their sharp edges. Each craftsman has his favourite tools and he uses them almost as a second set of fingers. Bamboo, too, is a hard wood, has a fine grain, and when sharply cut it is a pleasant and versatile pottery tool.

Experiments with tools to discover what they can or cannot do will prove to be fascinating and new uses for old tools will continually be found.

Loop-ended tools have a double usefulness: besides hollowing out the insides of models, they make crisp decorative patterns.

Useful decorating tools can be made from clay and when biscuit-fired are pleasant to work with. Rolls of clay can be cut into lengths of about 2″ and when leather-hard the ends can be decorated with simple designs. When they have been fired they can be pressed into the clay surface to produce interesting textures and patterns.

When initials are carved on the end these are called seals and are the mark the individual craftsman puts on to his pot to show he has made it. Any handmade pottery should bear one of these seals. To the potters of the East, these seal marks were very important, and were very carefully considered pieces of design.

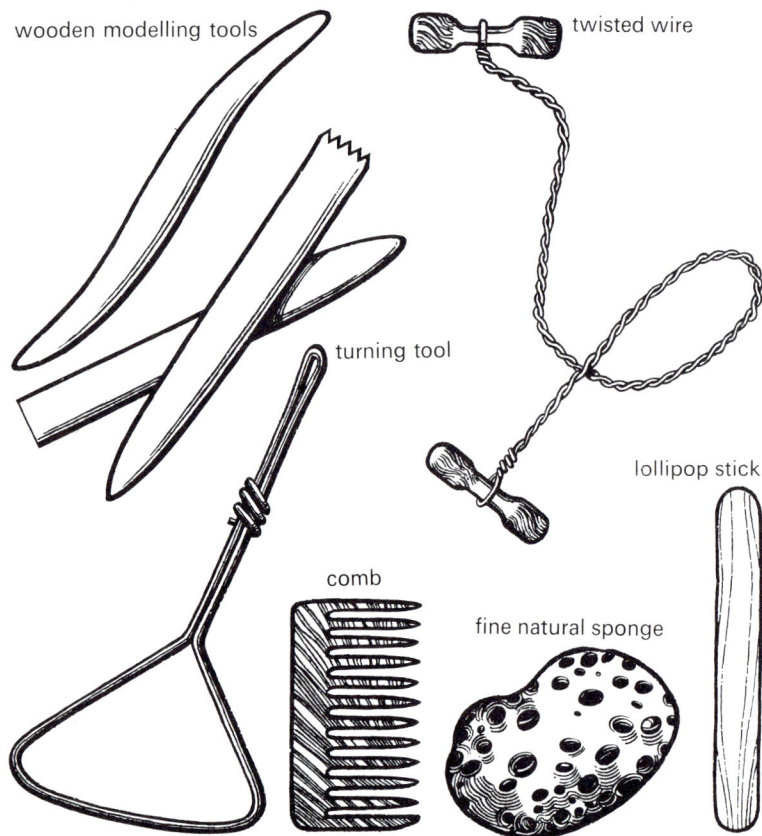

wooden modelling tools

twisted wire

turning tool

lollipop stick

comb

fine natural sponge

Early nineteenth century carpet balls.
Scottish

However, the tools used in the pottery should not be restricted to those listed in the supplier's catalogue, nor those made especially for the purpose. Rulers, keys, hacksaw blades, pen nib holders, lino-cutters, wooden stick-pattern makers, rings, cogs, etc., have all proved their worth and almost any fairly small simple shape is effective in producing some sort of pattern.

Bernard Leach describes decoration as being 'subordinate to form but intimately connected with it . . . and the question arises whether the increased orchestration adds to the total effect or not.'

3 Hand-built pottery

This chapter covers various aspects of pot-building which involve little or no equipment. The advantages of this are obvious and, as using the hands is of primary importance, the work is personal and very rewarding. Only when students have been introduced to clay through these simple processes should the more complicated techniques of moulding, and finally of throwing, be tackled.

It is certain that long before the wheel was invented, pots were built by hand. The simplest of these is in fact a thumb pot which, while being simple to make, demands a fair understanding of exactly what the clay will or will not do, and is capable of producing quite sophisticated designs.

Thumb pots

A thumb pot involves nothing other than the fingers and clay and the process is at once immediate and intimate. The technique is a skilled one and in Japan many beautiful bowls have been produced by this method for use during the tea ceremony, and are sometimes called pinch-pots.

a Simple ball of clay

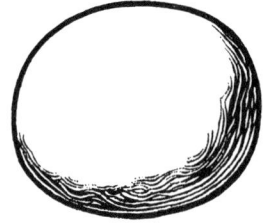

b Simple pot made by squeezing clay

c Thumb pot in progress

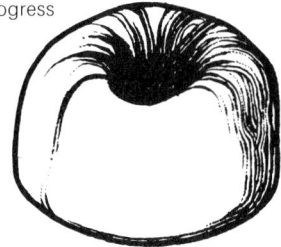

d Finished thumb pot

e Thumb pot with added foot ring

f One thumb pot cut in two halves, joined together and feet added

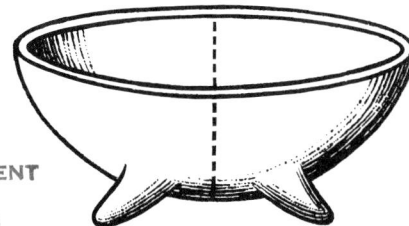

Thumb pots. Children 12

g Two thumb pots joined together with a hole in the top

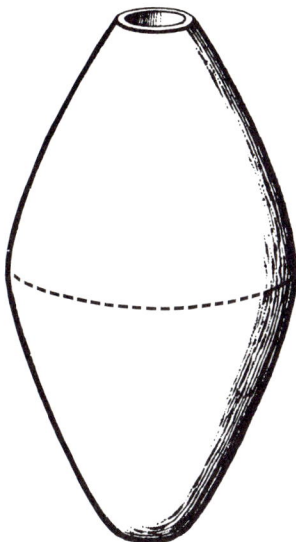

h A hanging plant pot formed from two thumb pots

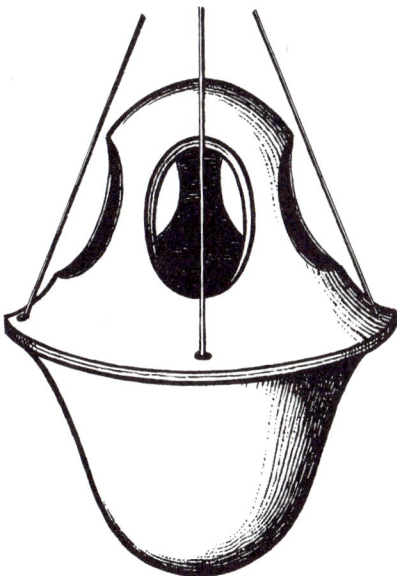

i Two thumb pots forming an egg shape. This can be beaten or squeezed into various shapes

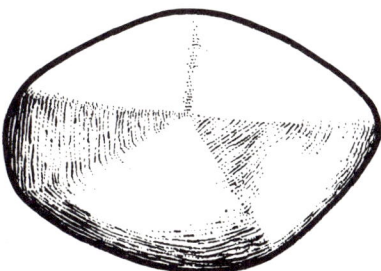

As an introduction to the technique of clay, these pots have several advantages. The process is similar in a way to that of thrown pottery except that on the wheel the clay goes round and the hands remain relatively still, while with thumb pots, the pot is revolved in the hands. The processes involved in throwing, such as centring, opening out and pulling upwards, can find their simple equivalent in the making of a thumb pot.

Again, because the thumb pot technique is something which can be developed without having to master and control mechanical equipment, results are fairly rapid and improvements can be noticed. The resulting pots offer ideal surfaces for experiments with many types of decoration.
Method
1. Prepare clay which should be softer than usual.
2. Knock a lump, about the size of a tennis ball, into a ball by passing it from hand to hand.
3. Hold the ball in one hand and press the thumb of the other hand exactly into the centre until it is about $\frac{1}{2}$" from the bottom.
4. Gently squeeze the clay between the fingers on the outside and the thumb on the inside, revolving the pot slowly.
5. Use the flat surface of the fingers and not the fingertips.
6. Keep the rim thicker than is finally intended. This gives the pot strength and helps to prevent it from flopping outwards and the rim from splitting.
7. Keep the pot in the hand all the time and if it has to be put down rest it on its rim.
8. Continue to squeeze the walls until they are about $\frac{3}{8}$" thick all over. The pressure should decrease as the pot progresses.
9. A simple border pattern can decorate the rim and can be made either by squeezing with the fingers, which is very difficult, or by using a tool.
10. The bottom of the pot can be trimmed with a knife if necessary when it has hardened slightly.
11. Any tendency for the pot to develop surface cracks could be due to several reasons:
 a. The clay was too hard to begin with.
 b. The pot has taken too long to make and the hands have dried out the surface.

If the hands are kept moist, rather than wet, the cracks on the surface will be eliminated. This is a more effective method than sponging the pot. Excessive water must be avoided or the clay will become too soft and the pot will collapse. Thumb pots must be made quickly and this is part of their attraction.

Coil pots

Perhaps one of the oldest and most versatile methods of pot-building is to join rolls of clay together. At one time they were joined together inside baskets and moulds and gradually a technique developed. Today the studio potter uses the technique and adds his own variations. The child finds great delight in rolling clay into sausages and building them up on top of each other to make a container. There are, of course, many methods of building coil pots and each potter swears by his own method; it is up to the individual to decide on the most effective method of working. The size of coil pots can vary from the smallest with the thinnest of walls to the largest pot conceivable. Again, the pots need not be confined to being round or even symmetrical at all, as thrown pots have to be. They can be oval, can be in the form of animals, birds or fish, they can have two necks, and so on; the range is almost limitless.

Method

1. Prepare clay ready for use.
2. The table should be clean and flat, with plenty of working space.
3. Use the reverse, unglazed side of a tile for supporting the base as, being slightly absorbent, it prevents the clay from sticking and cracking when drying.
4. Make the base by patting out a ball of clay with the edge of the hand; by turning the clay over and patting again, a really flat surface can be made. The base needs to be about $\frac{1}{2}$" thick. A base can also be made by using a rolling pin. There is no point in building up a base from coils.
5. Making coils:
a. The table must be clean and free from bits.
b. Work standing up, as it is much easier for maintaining a natural rhythm.
c. Squeeze clay into a sausage and roll between hands, keeping the ends pointed to prevent air bubbles.
d. Roll the sausage on the table using the palms and fingers of the hands.

Use the whole length of the hands from fingertips to wrists. It is important to rotate the coil at least $2\frac{1}{2}$ times at each rolling to ensure that it stays round—to allow the hands to see-saw slackly only results in an oval section which is inefficient and slows down the building of the walls. (The circumference of a circle is about three times as large as the diameter; from the formula $2\pi r$ (r=radius) the exact circumference of a coil can be worked out.

E.g. a coil with a radius of 1"

$$2 \times \tfrac{22}{7} \times 1 = \tfrac{44}{7} = 6\tfrac{2}{7}"$$

The circumference of a coil with a diameter of 1" is about 3".)
e. Keep the hands as parallel to the table as possible and the pressure gentle and even.
f. Start in the centre of the coil and move gradually outwards.

Coil pot with impressed decoration, and slip decoration. Child 15

Making coils

a coils

b base

c first coil in position

Coil built pot. Arizona
c AD 200

Hand-built burial urn, with a combination of applied
and incised decoration. Anglo-Saxon

Round-bottomed, hand-built cooking pot.
African

g. As a guide, coils need to be about $\frac{1}{2}$" thick though it obviously depends on the size of the pot.

6. Roll three or four coils before joining them together, so that a rhythm of work is established.

7. The coils need to have their hollow ends removed or flattened to eliminate any air which may have been trapped inside while rolling.

8. The first coil always goes directly on the edge of the base and is firmly pushed into place. A banding wheel, though not essential, is useful for working on and does help to keep a pot symmetrical, besides speeding up the work and making the adding of coils easier.

9. One coil should be put on at a time, pressed into position and firmly joined on to the one below. No slip need be used. The sides of the first coil should be pressed down on to the base both inside and out and the sides of the other coils pressed on to the coil immediately below.

10. To make the pot grow outwards, coils should be put on the outer edge of the coil below; to make it go inwards, they need to be put on the inner edge. At the beginning, coil pots have a tendency to go outwards and a simple, straight-sided cylinder is a good first exercise.

11. The inside should be smoothed off as much as possible while it is being built and the clay is soft: the finger is the most effective tool. The outside can be smoothed with the finger in the first place and when leather-hard it can be scratched first with the rough and then the smooth edge of a hacksaw blade. The rough edge goes through and not over the bumps and eventually removes them.

12. Often the pushing of one coil into another gives rise to a natural pattern which is often very pleasant to leave.

13. On a large pot it is only possible to build up three or four inches at a time, depending on the state of the clay. Only while the walls can stand the weight should more coils be added.

14. The rim needs to be kept damp and in the same state as the clay to be added on. This can be done by putting a damp strip of cloth round

the rim and covering the whole with polythene. The exact treatment depends on how long the pot is to be left in between sessions. It is often useful to have two pots on the go at the same time; one can be hardening while work goes on on the other. If the rim gets too hard it can be softened with a damp rag or scratched and slip applied before the new coil is added. This is the only time that slip is used.

15. Pot tapping: Gentle tapping on the side of a pot with a flat wooden surface, e.g. wooden spoon, has three purposes:
   a. knocks the coils together,
   b. smooths the sides of the pot,
   c. gives the desired shape.

   The tapping must be done systematically and before the walls have become too hard. Each profile of the pot should be tapped and a banding wheel makes this much more effective, especially if it is done at eye level. The inside of the pot can be tapped out with a pestle, but this needs to be done carefully or the pot may split.

16. The top of the pot can be trimmed when necessary if it gets uneven. Place the pot centrally on a banding wheel and hold it in position with rolls of clay. A fine wire should be stretched across one wall of the pot at right angles to it. Revolve the turntable and hold the wire firm, and turn the top down until it is flat all round. A similar method is to use a needle in a cork. The wheel is revolved quickly and the needle held to the surface to give a clean crisp line. The surplus can be cut away.

17. The final stage of the pot is important and demands careful consideration. One of the advantages the coil pot has over the thrown pot is that various stages can be considered separately. The top or rim must be in character with the way the pot has been built. For example, a fairly large coil pot will need a top with a bold and final quality about it, while the rim should be at least the thickness of the walls.

18. The same ideas about decoration apply equally to coil and any other pots. It must be a natural outcome of the form and complement it. Any of the methods of decoration mentioned earlier in Chapter 2 are suitable, either singly or in combination. One danger which must be watched is that large coil pots tend to get very hard and this makes it difficult to add clay decoration to the sides. Coil pots have an almost limitless range to offer the enterprising craftsman, both in methods of working and in the variety of pots which can be made. The coils can be added and then thrown on a kickwheel to give a very smooth and controlled method of working, though this is a technique for more advanced students. The main point seems to be the pleasantness of the work. It is quiet and rhythmical and there is plenty of opportunity to study and control the form as it develops.

Slab pots

At a recent meeting of potters there was a discussion about slab pots (pots built out of flat slabs of clay), and whether they could be called by a more attractive name. No one had any really original or satisfactory ideas, so they remain slab pots: the name sounds dull and uninviting, yet

Trimming the uneven top from a coil pot

pot on centre

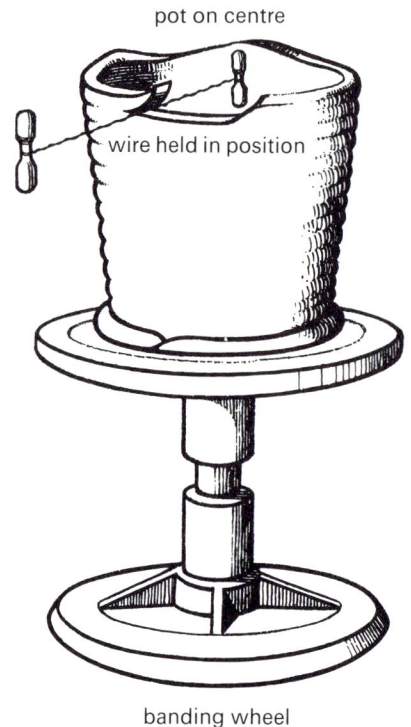

wire held in position

banding wheel

Unglazed slab pot. Child 15

Slab pots of various shapes

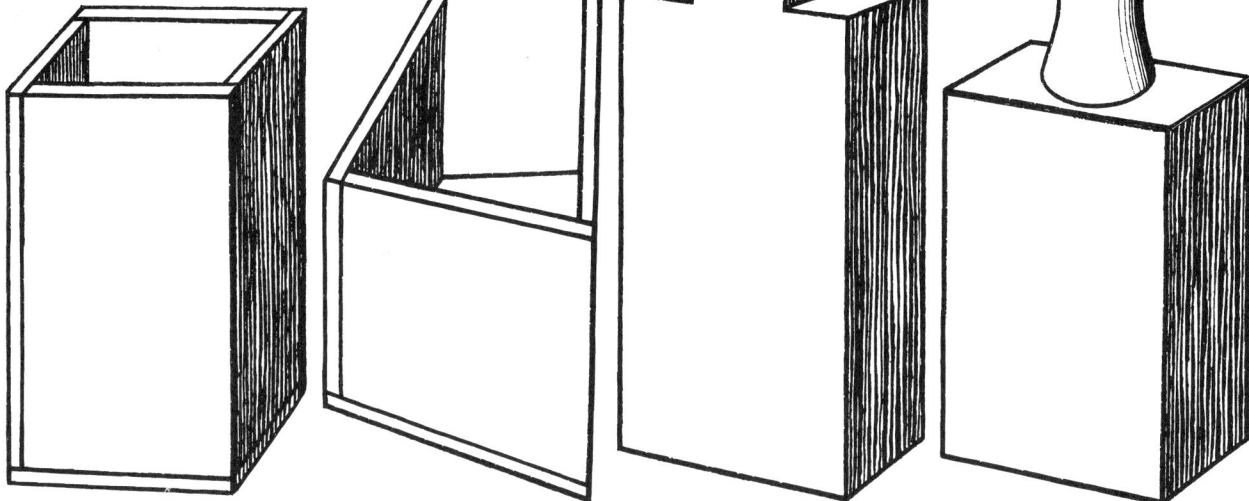

the technique, when developed, can produce graceful, sophisticated pots such as those by Shoji Hamada in Japan and George Feathers in England. Slab pots have a character and style of their own; one of the most satisfactory ways of making a pot with sharp edges is to use slabs of clay joined together. On the other hand, slabs need not always remain flat and are capable of being twisted and curved to give exciting results, besides which the slabs can be cut and decorated before being used. The technique is, in fact, a sort of ceramic carpentry.

(Mould pots are simply slabs of clay which take on the shape of the mould, and will be dealt with in Chapter 5.)

Method

Different potters have their own individual method of joining slabs together, and again it is up to the individual to decide on the most suitable method, but there are certain points which need to be watched.

1. The slabs of clay to be joined should be, as far as possible, in the same state of hardness. Softer clay has a better chance of forming a good join than hard clay but there is a higher risk of damage and warping, so a happy medium has to be found, usually depending on the size of the pot.

2. The slabs need normally to be sufficiently hard to withstand their own weight; when this is not possible, some sort of temporary prop is needed.

3. Scoring both surfaces to be joined helps, though some potters say it is unnecessary. Slip should be used in any case.

4. Both surfaces need to be pressed firmly together and moved up and down slightly so that they bite.

5. Outside walls may need supporting with buttresses of clay or bricks to prevent collapse or distortion.

6. Tall pots should stand on the largest side.

7. It is easier to make slabs out of soft clay but these should be allowed to harden slightly before the final shape is cut as soft clay is quickly pulled out of shape.

8. The slabs can be made by one of two methods, usually depending on how many slabs are required.

Method 1 is good when only a few slabs are required and merely consists of rolling out the clay, rather like pastry. A full description of this method can be found in Chapter 5.

Method 2 is suitable when a quantity of slabs are required, and consists of slicing a brick of clay up with a wire.

a. Two measuring sticks, about 14" long, with saw cuts at $\frac{1}{8}$" intervals along one side, are required.

b. A twisted wire with loops or wooden handles on the end, is stretched between the two sticks and the wire is pushed through the block of clay, starting from the bottom.

c. The wire is moved from one cut to the next and the thickness of the slabs can vary from $\frac{1}{8}$" upwards. $\frac{3}{8}$" is a good thickness for average-sized pots.

d. The slabs can be spread out on a flat surface to dry and can be decorated with incised decoration before they are put into position. This allows quite complicated and bold decorations to be carved out. The twisted wire does give a slightly textured surface which is pleasant, though it can easily be removed by gently rolling the hardened clay with a rolling pin. This also evens out any bumps caused by handling the soft clay, though the rolling must be done carefully as the slabs must be the same thickness all over or uneven drying or warping will result.

Cutting the slabs

a. All the slabs must be at the same degree of hardness both when they are cut and when they are joined together.

b. Templates, made out of lino, cardboard or even out of paper, provide a useful guide and ensure that the sizes are calculated before cutting begins.

c. A metal rule and a sharp edge make cutting much easier. The cutting tool must be held absolutely vertically, and the cut should be on the waste side of the clay, with the rule resting on the part required.

Building with slabs

Boxes can be built in slabs and children often find this a useful introduction to the technique, but they should move on to more adventurous work. Here is a list of suggested ideas for the use of slabs:

1. Small box with lid.

a. Draw up templates and work out sizes.

b. Rest the sides on top of the base.

c. The lid should have a flange which fits snugly inside the base. A knob will only be required if the lid is too large to lift comfortably.

d. The joins can be strengthened by the addition of a thin coil of clay.

2. Other geometrical shaped boxes.

a. Triangular boxes are tricky because the joints have to be cut at an angle, though these could be calculated in a maths lesson.

b. Round boxes have a pleasant quality, though small ones are very tricky as the clay tends to split. When clay is bent it must be on the soft side.

3. Slabs can be wrapped round cylinders, such as pieces of scaffolding, to make long thin pots. Newspaper put round the post first will prevent the clay from sticking and allow it to slide off easily. This is important

Slicing clay to make slabs

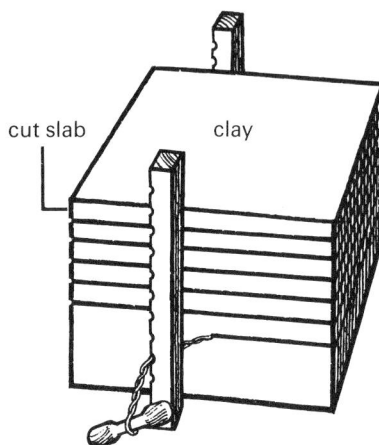

cut slab   clay

sticks with notches to guide wire

Clay slab wrapped round a rolling pin

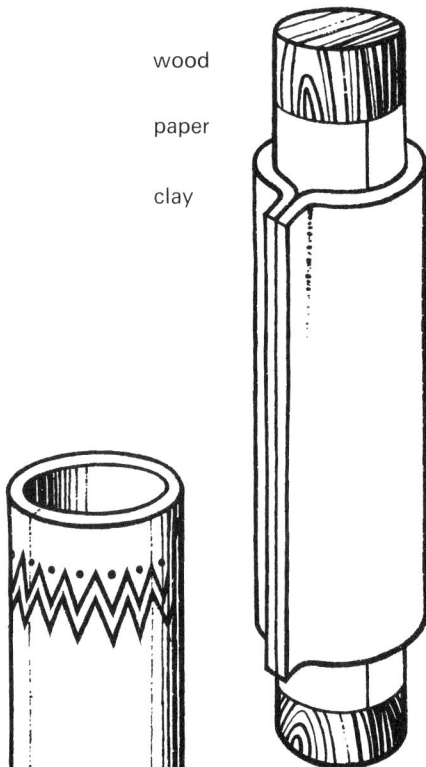

wood

paper

clay

Incised decoration on a slab pot

as the pot must be removed fairly quickly, because as the clay dries and contracts it will split or crack open. Any paper which sticks to the clay will dry off or be burnt away during the biscuit firing.

4. Medium size cylindrical pots can be made without a guide, though again the clay must be soft.

When making the tall round pots, the two edges must of course, be joined together as firmly as possible both on the inside and on the out- side; there is no reason why the join should not form a dominant part of the pattern; the inside join can be reinforced with a thin coil of clay when possible, though this must be throughly smoothed in. On the long narrow pots a long stick can be used to push the internal joints together and smooth them over.

As a general rule, sides should always be put on top of a base and the joins made as firmly as possible, as the major weakness of slab pots is their tendency to warp out of position or to split at the joins, either while drying or during the firing. Allow slab pots to dry out slowly; this will help reduce the danger of warping. Finally, joins can be made crisper by cleaning them carefully with the smooth side of a piece of a hacksaw blade while they are still leather-hard.

The edges of the slab are very important, they determine the whole character of the pot and it should be decided at the beginning whether or not they are going to be left clean or made round and smooth. Soft slabs can be pinched together to form a pot, though again there must be a rhythm about any marks left which will give the pot its character.

It is possible to combine building with slabs with other methods of pot building. Coils can be built on to bases formed out of slabs or thrown necks can be luted on to form bottles of various sizes. Again, the range is endless and, as work progresses, many variations will suggest themselves.

Pots with incised decoration, made by wrapping slabs of clay round cardboard tubes. Children 14

The flat surfaces associated with slab pots are, of course, eminently suitable for decoration of all kinds. It can be pressed into the soft clay or painted or trailed on in the form of slip; it can be painted on in underglaze or even added with enamels.

Tiles

Tiles are simply flat slabs of clay and their main joy for the potter is the perfect surface they offer for decoration. The main difficulty about tile-making is preventing the tile warping out of shape. Commercial tiles are produced under pressure by machinery from dry powdered clay and remain perfectly flat. (It is the drying process which causes the warping.) Although this cannot be done in the studio, there are various ways in which one can help to prevent warping:

1. The body must be fairly open. An addition of up to 25 per cent grog helps greatly, both by assisting even drying and by reducing the amount the body will contract.
2. Slow, even drying is essential with, if possible, the tiles being turned frequently.
3. The tiles must not be too large (a 6″ square is a good size), nor must they be too thin, $\frac{1}{2}$″ the minimum thickness.

Tiles can be made in several ways:

1. Clay can be rolled out and cut to form the tile.
2. If tiles of the same size are required, they need to be made in a wooden box—see diagram. The clay can be pressed in and the surface either scraped or rolled flat.

   The backs of the tiles need to be roughened if they are to be cemented into position when finished.

   As clay contracts while drying, tiles being made to a definite size for a particular purpose must have the shrinkage of the clay calculated and this must be allowed for. Most clays shrink by about one-eighth from their original damp state. The initial shrinkage occurs during drying and again while being fired. The exact shrinkage rate of any clay can be calculated by the following method:

a. Out of medium soft clay make several lengths about 6 in. long and 1 in. wide and $\frac{1}{2}$ in. thick.
b. Mark, with a sharp edge, a length of five inches on one side of each length.
c. Dry them carefully and slowly, turning them frequently to avoid warping.
d. Take a measurement of the marks at various stages:
 (i) leather-hard
(ii) dry
(iii) after being biscuit-fired
(iv) after being in a glaze firing (see Chapter 8).
e. Compare these measurements and notice when most shrinkage takes place. The total percentage shrinkage can be calculated from this simple formula:

$$\text{Shrinkage} = \frac{\text{plastic length minus fired length}}{\text{plastic length}} \times 100$$

Tile box: home made

Tile box: factory made

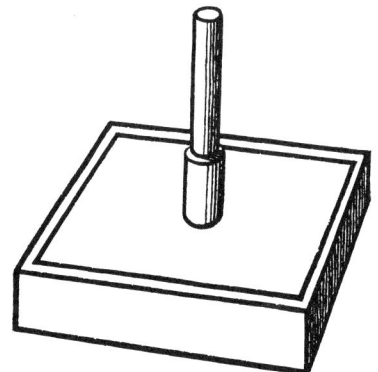

Encaustic tiles with inlay of white slip. Early
English, fourteenth century

Tiles with impressed decoration. Children 12

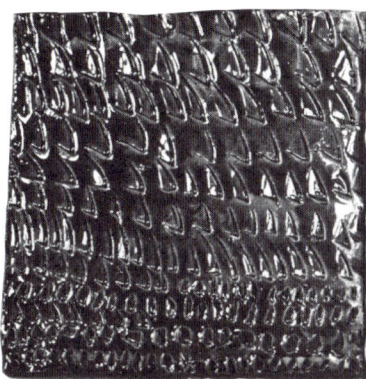

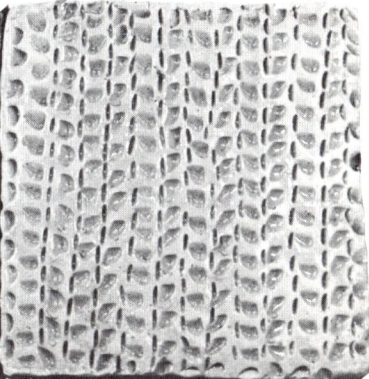

Tiles with geometrical applied decoration.
Children 13

Left: tile with inlay of white slip. Child 15
Right: tile with incised decoration painted
with oxides. Child 12

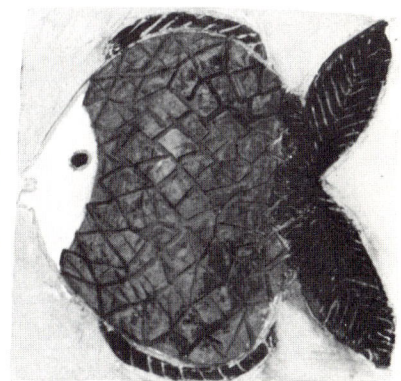

Tiles have the great advantage of demanding decoration. This can be done on the raw clay with incised decoration, or the tiles can form the basis of modelled decoration. Slip can be used, or the tiles can be biscuit fired and colour can be painted on. These techniques are described in the chapter on glazing. The tiles need not be square, but can be almost any geometrical shape.

The mediaeval potters, especially the monks working in monastic potteries, produced encaustic tiles. These were, simply, slabs of clay with fairly deep impressions made on the surface, which were filled with clay of a different colour. This clay was probably added in the form of slip. As the tiles were intended to be walked upon, the design did not wear off as the tiles wore down. Beautiful examples of these tiles can be found in the Chapter Houses of York Minster and Westminster Abbey. The simple designs and motives which were employed were very pleasant and lively. Here is a simple method of making these tiles:

1. The original tile is made first with the design carved into it.
2. A plaster mould of this is then taken.
3. The original is removed and the mould used to produce more tiles.
4. The impression is filled up with either poured, painted or trailed slip. Several layers may be necessary.
5. When leather-hard, any raised slip can be scraped away with a sharp flat edge pulled across the surface.

4 Modelling

Heads intended to show exaggerated emotions. Children 12

Modelling in clay is a direct means of expressing feelings and using the imagination. Like all forms of pottery, modelling involves three-dimensional form, and therefore the consideration of every profile; this means that the work must constantly be turned round and examined, one part in relationship to the other. Modelling is the process whereby clay is added, taken away, or redistributed while carving is the process whereby clay is cut or carved away only, and can be done very successfully with clay which is in a leather or cheese-hard state.

Modelling is an activity quite distinct from making pots, although making pots often involves modelling. Modelling must, however, also follow the basic limitations of clay, as these can dictate the most suitable forms. These are some of the facts one must take into account:

1. Large pieces of clay protruding from the main body are difficult to construct and weak when finished.
2. Thin, spindly legs supporting a large body are virtually impossible to construct and, if achieved, look weak and are fragile.
3. Clay provides an excellent surface for texture and for fine, precise detail.
4. Work can be kept damp and can therefore be considered over a period of time.
5. It can also be allowed to dry out to allow the carving of fine detail.
6. As long as modelling in clay is not confused with producing perfect reproductions of natural objects or even porcelain figures, and the idea is carried out in the terms imposed by the clay, then the results are likely to be good.

Good pictures or photographs of, for example, animals, act both as a source of inspiration and supply basic information for modelling, though it is the artist's job to adapt and interpret the photograph or picture in terms of clay.

Listed are the various techniques which are in common use and these, in themselves, may stimulate ideas. They may, of course, be used in conjunction with each other.

1 Pulling

A lump of clay is pulled, pushed, knocked and rolled into shape. The solid shape can later be hollowed out from the base, using a loop-ended wire tool. Animals and simple figures are obvious examples, and the pulling and stroking of parts of the clay can result in a strong feeling of movement.

As an exercise in the control of a clay lump, it can be knocked into a cube, rolled into a cylinder, made into a ball, pyramid, etc., before being pulled.

2 Coiled models

The basic shape of many models can be built up this way; for example, animals, figures, fish. The technique is perhaps better suited to large models; the inside can either be left with the coils showing, or smoothed over. No base is necessary, only a rim on a tile or a batt. The coils tend to impose their own basic form so it is often necessary to simplify the form in order to make the technique work. This demands careful observation

Snake. Child 13

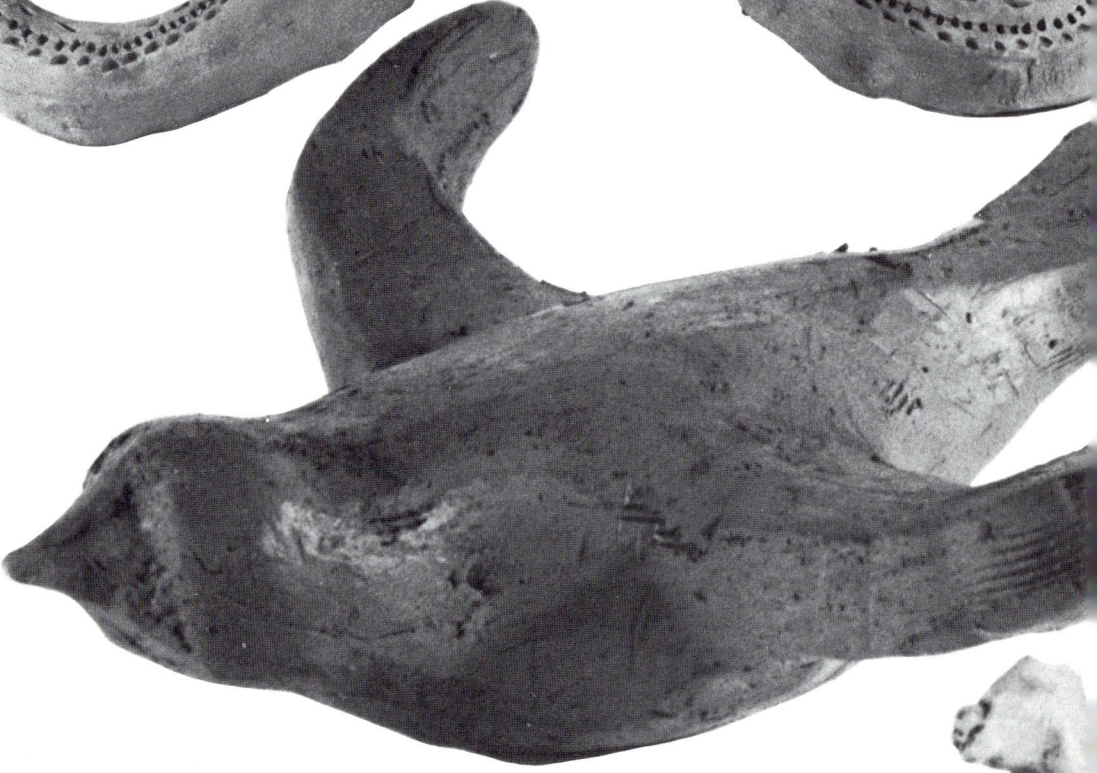

Bird. Child 15

Imaginary animal. Child 11

of the main characteristics of, say, an animal, if the result is to be success-ful.

The outside of the body can be modelled and if necessary large pieces added to it. The body itself is built up in exactly the same way as an ordinary coil pot, described in Chapter 3.

3 Sculpture

Using a support or armature, large figures can be built up without the limitations imposed by the clay. Strictly speaking, this is outside the realm of either pottery or modelling, and is an entirely separate art form. It demands great skill, and while there is no reason why experiments should not be made using an armature, the following points need to be borne in mind:

a. As clay dries it loses water and so contracts in size; therefore it may crack away from the armature and probably disintegrate.

b. Clay with foreign bodies of any kind, if allowed to dry, cannot be fired. If the actual modelling did not crack during drying, it certainly would during a firing, and any metal would melt. The only ways to make a sculpture of this kind permanent, are:

   (i) cast it in plaster while it is still damp (which is a complicated technical skill), or

   (ii) in the case of a bust, to remove it from the armature by slicing it down the middle, hollow out the inside, and join the two halves together. Repair work can cover up the join. The neck should be left hollow and, after drying out, the bust should be fired slowly. Afterwards a block of wood set in plaster in the inside of the head acts as a sufficient support fixed to the base.

4 Slabs

1. Pieces of clay rolled out flat do not necessarily have to be left flat or, in fact, be made into slab pots. Slabs can be made using the method described in the section on Slab Pots in Chapter 3, and then curled round, twisted or bent to form cones, cylinders, which can form the basis of, say, a figure. This is especially good for building up figures or models to a good height, which is often difficult for children.

2. The first operation can be explained and some sort of guide given about the size to work to, and the basic body shape can be made very rapidly. It is often much easier to work on a base, which is easily built, than it is to start from a very solid lump of clay, waiting for inspiration.

3. For the more mechanically minded the slabs can be used for building houses or forts, the actual measurements can be used as a basis and a scale model can be produced. Forts, houses and Greek temples have been produced by this method. There are here obviously useful links to be made with both mathematics and history.

4. From the flat slabs of clay, figures can be cut almost as silhouettes, then modelling can be done on the surface.

5 Hollowing out

Thumb pots, described in Chapter 3, can be joined together to form heads, simple animals, such as pigs, hedgehogs, or the solid forms can be hollowed out as mentioned in method 1 for pulled shapes. These points are worth noting:

Mother and child modelled from slabs. Child 17

1. Solid lumps need to be hollowed out, both as an economy measure to save clay and as a precaution against the clay exploding during firing. Any thickness of clay over 2″ is a firing risk, as moisture can easily become trapped, and takes a long time to dry out.
2. Two methods of hollowing out:
a. Using a wire-ended modelling tool from the base.
b. Cutting the model in two with a wire, hollowing out both sections, leaving a wall at least $\frac{1}{2}$″ thick and as even as possible, and joining the two halves back together with slip. A small hole left at the base will allow the air to expand inside the pot, though this can be made after any re-modelling has been done, as the air trapped inside will prevent the sides from being pushed in.

6 Thrown and luted forms

Pots thrown on the wheel can act as a base for modelled work, besides which pots can be cut and joined together. Throwing imposes a strong character on the shapes, which can be exciting and highly individual. Naturally this technique is for those who have good control over throwing and can master the desired shapes.

7 Relief modelling

Modelling on a flat surface presents its own problems and lends itself both to realistic and more textured, abstract work.

Figures can be modelled either individually or on a slab of clay. Large tiles which fit together can be built individually. There is a limit to the size these can be made, as they tend to warp during drying or split during firing. Clay used should contain about 10 per cent grog to reduce shrinkage, and should be dried out very slowly and evenly, and not left in a warm room so that the edges dry rapidly and curl up.

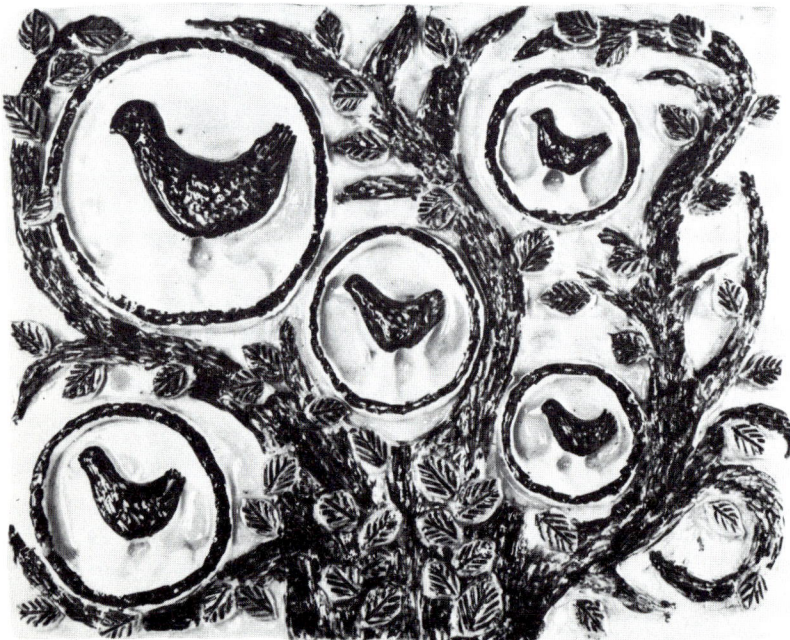

Panel using birds as a decorative theme. Child 17

If large decorative panels are being made, the joins should fit in with the natural divisions in the pattern or design.

Slabs of clay can be cut into, left flat, and decorated with underglaze, enamels, or slip, or modelled. The range is large and the chance for experiment great. Problems of decorating large areas with only slight and often subtle surface changes present plenty of problems, and so the bold, larger-than-life kind of decoration is perhaps more successful. It is a useful technique for combining art and pottery work; the designs can be worked out beforehand in the art class.

Clays of different colours can be used together and simple colour changes effected. A slip consisting of equal parts of the two bodies can be used for luting them together but care must be taken to keep the colours separate and the work clean, as it quickly becomes untidy and messy. Red terra cotta clay has a particularly strong staining effect on white clay which is difficult to remove.

As far as figures go, the range is large, and the method has the enormous advantage of not having to deal with the technical problem of making the clay stand upright. Full consideration can be given to the figures and how to obtain a three-dimensional look on a flat surface. Many kinds of tools can be used to suggest the various textures of the clothes and materials used: careful studies can be made of historical costume. Each child can work on his own figure and an effective group can be built up. One of the most useful ways in which depth can be suggested is by putting one thing behind the other.

8 Mosaics

Strictly speaking, the technique of mosaic does not really come into pottery, but may interest some children. The technique, simply, is to put small pieces of different coloured materials together, in such a way that the effect is made by the whole. At various times, marbles of many colours and stones have been used. Tesserae, the name given to the small individual parts, can be made in clay, glazed, and fitted together. Pots, broken down into small pieces, can also be used. Bits of pot can be prevented from flying about when being broken up, if the pot is covered with a towel or some strong material. Making tesserae is a long and often tedious process, but if a large group of children are working, the amount required can be produced. Care must be taken to ensure they are all of the same thickness, so that the finished surface will be more or less level.

The easiest way is to slice the clay using the sticks and wire method (Chapter 5), allow the slabs to dry slightly, and then cut them up into shapes with sides of about $\frac{1}{2}$". Glazing tends to be tedious, but if each is dipped carefully in the glaze so that the top surface and a small part of the sides is covered, no fettling (cleaning of the glaze) is needed, and it can be placed directly on to the kiln shelf, and thus time will be saved. A wide range of colour is required for mosaics, especially of each particular shade, so that depth can be achieved.

Mosaics can be fitted together inside a frame and then plaster of Paris put into the cracks. Alternatively, after being fitted together, a sheet of paper can be pasted over the top, the lot turned over so that the backs are showing, and plaster poured over. When dry, the paper can be soaked off, and the mosaic should be set hard and fast.

36

Finishing models

It is debatable whether models should be glazed, or left in their biscuit state. There is no simple right or wrong; it depends upon the particular work. Red clay, when fired to 1100°C. does have a pleasant quality and colour which rarely needs glazing, and unless an opaque glaze is used, any other will give a dark effect. Grey clays, however, do not have this rich quality, and generally need some kind of finish. This should be borne in mind when the work starts, and the clay chosen accordingly.

Working notes

1. Fine detailed modelling is easily obscured by glaze and so is normally worked in red clay and left unglazed.
2. White clay forms a good body for coloured and transparent glazes, which tend to settle in grooves and any impressed decoration, and gives a dark, richer effect. This quality can be exploited on some kinds of modelling.
3. As a rule, unglazed clay has a rougher, more primitive quality, as opposed to the more sophisticated glazed and decorated ware.
4. Work glazed with a white tin opaque glaze and then decorated, must rely upon the painting for effect, so the forms need to be simple and uncluttered.

The results can be bright and colourful, and contrast pleasantly with unglazed ware. Examples of this work can be seen in the Staffordshire figures of the late eighteenth century and nineteenth century. The colours can be used in a naturalistic or more abstract way, but they must be chosen carefully. Some models lend themselves to an all-over glaze, while others do not.

Flat surfaces, of course, can have any desired decorative combination; some parts can be glazed and others left raw.

Chimney ornament 'Adam and Eve'. Staffordshire c 1745

Below left: musician playing a violin. English, c 1750

Below centre: thrown and modelled pot in the shape of a woman. English c 1740

Below: Mochica warrior. Peruvian c AD 600

Right: ornamental brick house. Chinese c 215

Below: T'ang horse

Below right: bullock cart. Chinese sixth century

Below: man feeding bird. Early Chinese

5 Moulds

Moulds are used in industry for the mass-production of utility ware, and pottery has been specially designed to be produced by this method. This process has little in common with studio pottery, though some of its techniques are very useful in the studio. In school, moulds are a very convenient way of making simple flat dishes which cannot be made in any other way and also allow many pots suitable for different types of design to be made fairly quickly. Pots made in a mould should have a quality of their own, and not be imitations of pots produced by other methods. It is possible, for example, for a round pot to be made in a mould, but it can be made much more quickly and with more character on a wheel. Moulding is a recognised industrial technique but it has little value for the craftsman. In the classroom, pots which are asymmetrical are the type most suitable for reproduction in a mould.

Only the simplest moulds need be the concern of this book. More complicated moulds require a highly skilled knowledge and considerable time and energy in their manufacture with results which often prove to be of no creative value when all the work has been done.

Moulds were probably used for some of the first pots to be made. Clay, smeared on the inside of a basket, allowed to dry and fired in a bonfire, would produce a pot. So would clay built up round a stone or put on the inside of a gourd or shell. Coils can be built up round wooden blocks, and provided the block is removed before the clay dries and shrinks, simple but effective pots can be made quickly. These provide an excellent basis for decoration and for further building.

Coils built round a square mould

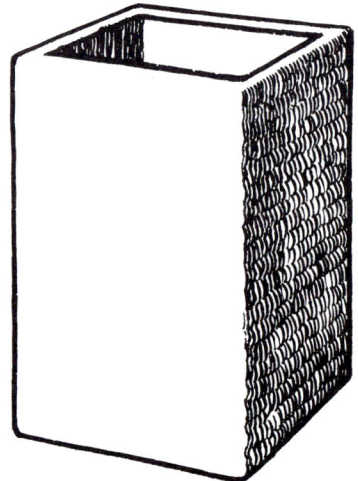

Left: Aretine mould, made in clay and biscuit fired. First century BC

Egyptian
hollow moulds

a Clay model

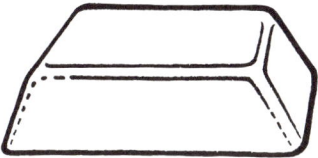

b Making a plaster casting mould

wall of clay or lino

glass or paper

Plastic bowls of about 6″ diameter provided the moulds for the pots illustrated on page 45. Soft clay rolled out into slabs about $\frac{3}{8}$″ thick was liberally sprinkled with flint to prevent it sticking to the smooth surface of the bowls. These were either laid over or on the inside of the moulds, were removed as soon as possible and stood on their rims to harden. When leather-hard they were decorated to provide a wide variety of bowls from the same mould.

A one-piece mould, into which a slab of clay is laid, is perhaps the most useful to the craftsman. Its manufacture is simple, and the low dishes it can produce are eminently suitable as a basis for experiments with decoration and design. These moulds form a part of the tradition of English pottery, and photographs or drawings of these pots should be constantly referred to. Traditionally they were decorated with slip patterns and the combination of white and coloured slips on the terra cotta body was often a very successful one.

From a teacher's, as well as from a potter's, point of view it is more satisfactory and more pleasing if the whole process of making moulds and pressing dishes is carried out by the same person. Naturally, this can present plenty of problems in a school where space is often restricted, but two students can work on one mould and, when the whole process has been completed, then the moulds can be used by other students and the emphasis put on decoration.

Press-in or hollow moulds

A press-in mould is simply a plaster block with a hollow, into which a flat piece of clay is pressed.

Method

1. A model must first be made in solid clay. This shape must have neither undercutting nor sharp corners. The first model especially should have a plain shape and it is often useful to base it on a simple geometrical shape rather than attempt a complicated twisting design.
2. As a rough guide, the model should be no less than 2″ and no more than 4″ deep. This will enable clay to be pressed into the mould easily and can dry without warping. The first model should not be too large in length and breadth, say 5″ to 10″, though with experience the size can be increased to 2′.
3. If the model is built up on a smooth, flat surface, it will ensure that the plaster comes away easily and evenly—glass is very good and so is perspex or plastic, which, being slightly flexible, does help. A margin of 2″ needs to be left round the model. Other points are:
   a. No sharp corners.
   b. No right angles.
   c. No undercutting.
   d. The edges should be crisp and clean where they touch the base.
   e. The surface should be as smooth as possible. If the clay is fairly soft it can be modelled easily and as it hardens, it can be smoothed flat with a hacksaw blade by the method used for smoothing the outside of coil pots.
4. When the model has been prepared, a wall of either clay or lino should be built round it. This needs to be about 1″ from the model and 1″ above it. The wall must be strong and plaster-proof and all joins should

be smoothed over with clay to prevent plaster seeping through. Stout cord round a lino wall will help to prevent it from opening under the weight of the plaster. Clay walls need to be buttressed with either bricks or lumps of clay. If the glass is painted with a layer of slip it will help to prevent the plaster sticking.

5. Mixing the plaster:

a. If the mould is not too large the whole amount of plaster can be mixed in one operation.

b. Estimate the amount of plaster required and put the appropriate amount of water into a bowl. A plastic bowl will allow any hardened plaster to be removed easily.

c. Sprinkle the plaster into the water until little mountains appear above the surface. Never add water to plaster and try to avoid dropping the plaster in large quantities which may trap in air and make mixing difficult.

d. Agitate the mixture by shaking your hand underneath the surface, so causing the plaster to mix and air bubbles to rise to the surface. Gently stir the plaster until it is smooth, even and creamy. If a layer of clean water appears on the surface this must be removed or more plaster added quickly.

e. After a few minutes, the time depending on the plaster, the mixture will begin to stiffen and it should be poured into the mould at this point. The plaster needs to cover the model by about $\frac{3}{4}''$.

f. If the model is large and two layers of plaster have to be mixed, the first coat must be roughened before it sets and dampened before the second layer is added.

g. To give the mould a flat, even base, gently tap the board on which it has been made before the plaster sets and the plaster will even out.

h. Great care must be taken when disposing of plaster waste. Any surplus plaster should be put into the waste bin and not down the sink as this will quickly block up the drain. It is useful to have an efficient waste trap over the plughole to prevent any trouble, rather than trying to cure it when it has happened.

i. When the plaster begins to crystallize and harden, it loses its shiny surface and after a few more minutes it begins to generate heat; then the supporting walls can be carefully removed, and any sharp edges gently smoothed over, though it is not advisable to handle the mould yet as it is still fragile. The initials or name of the person making the mould could be scratched on to the back at this stage if desired.

j. Clay which has come into contact with the plaster should never be mixed with the ordinary clay, if the risk of contamination is to be avoided. Plaster in clay is one of the potter's enemies, as it causes pots to crack either before or during firing because of its high absorption rate or, as it melts at a fairly low temperature, it can run out on to the surface of the pot and cause a nasty and unwelcome mess. Either a special bin should be kept for contaminated clay or it should be thrown away.

k. After about half an hour, the model can be removed from the plaster by being gently prised out, as the clay will probably have absorbed moisture from the plaster. This is not difficult. Plaster never sticks to damp clay. The mould needs to dry out for a day or two before use.

c Plaster mould

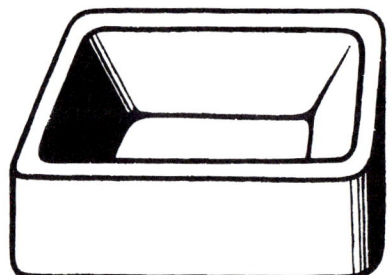

Care of plaster

There are many grades of plaster of Paris and they are priced according to their fineness. Ordinary plaster is suitable for school moulds and is much cheaper purchased by the hundredweight but, if really fine, small moulds are required, dental plaster can be purchased from chemists. Plaster needs to be stored in an airtight container in a dry place to prevent it absorbing moisture, as this causes it to loose its setting powers. If plaster has been stored for a long time it may need sieving if it is lumpy and a small quantity should be tested to ensure that it has not lost its setting powers.

Filling the mould

1. *Rolling out clay*

a. Prepare the clay thoroughly, having it slightly softer than normal.

b. Roll the clay out on deck-chair canvas or hessian to prevent it from sticking and for ease of lifting it into position. Hessian gives a rough texture and canvas a fine texture to the clay.

c. Rolling guides can be used to ensure a good even thickness, which is very important, as uneven thicknesses of clay dry out and contract differently and warping of the dish will occur. With practice the guides can be dispensed with.

d. Knock the lump of clay fairly flat in the middle of the canvas before rolling starts, as it makes the process easier. Turning the clay over will also assist this operation.

e. *Always* start rolling from the centre of the clay outwards and roll right off it. Do not roll back, but lift the rolling pin back to the centre of the clay and roll out again. The aim is to push the clay outwards and if the rolling pin is rolled back, the clay tends to curl round it and mess up the process. It is much easier to roll away from you than towards you, so turning the canvas round and rolling the other half of the clay is much more satisfactory. Both hands should be used for rolling and the pressure should be near the guides. For this reason, a broom handle is not so satisfactory as it is not sufficiently rigid when pressure is put on it. Ensure that sufficient clay has been rolled out to fit the mould and cut away any obviously spare clay.

Clay suitable for putting into moulds can either be rolled out, as described above, or it can be sliced with wire when several slabs are required. This method is described fully in the section on slab pottery (Chapter 3).

2. *Putting the clay in the mould*

A small bowl of water, a soft sponge, and a wire cutter, will be required.

a. Remove the clay from the canvas by lifting the canvas and slipping a hand underneath the clay. When larger slabs are made this method is not practicable, especially if the clay is soft. In this case, the canvas can be lifted and the mould lifted so that the canvas is reversed over the mould. This means that the texture of the canvas will be on the inside and not on the outside of the dish. If the dish is fairly shallow, the slab can be allowed to harden slightly before being handled, which makes reversing it much easier.

d Rolling out clay

b. Once in the mould, the slab should be eased gently into position with a damp sponge. Fingertip pressure must be avoided as this tends to dent the clay rather than press it against the mould sides. Avoid wetting the surface excessively.

c. Most of the surplus clay can be cut away with the wire cutter before the edges are finally trimmed. Ensure that the clay has filled every part of the mould and the surface is as smooth as possible before final trimming takes place. The final trim is very important as it gives the dish its rim which in turn makes the pot look strong or weak. The rim should be a neat, flat edge level with the top of the mould. A fine wire should be held taut at right angles to the wall and pulled towards the corners, not away from them. This prevents the corners being pulled out of shape.

d. If a rounded, instead of a flat rim is wanted, this can be sponged round after the dish has got to the leather-hard stage and has been removed from the mould. It is unwise to remove the dish before it has got to the leather-hard stage or it may go out of shape, or even collapse. Dishes are normally decorated while they are still in the mould and always so decorated when slip is being used.

Decoration of mould pots

1. Incised or pressed decoration is done while the pot is still leather-hard. It is a method of decoration which shows up very well on a light body under a transparent glaze. The method is dealt with in Chapter 4.

2. Slip decoration is the most traditional method and is very effective. There are many ways in which slip can be used and applied. The directions for mixing slip can be found in Chapter 3.

e Easing clay into mould

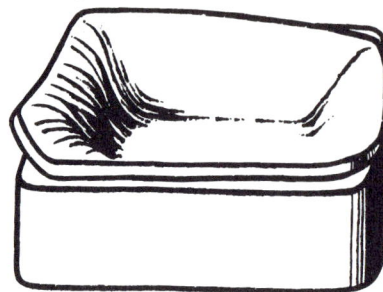

f Cutting away surplus clay

g Finished pot

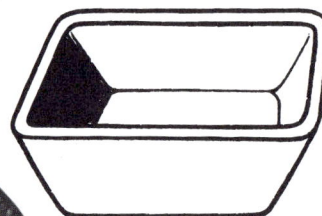

Slipware baking dish made from a mould. Tichnall, Derbyshire, dated 1787

Mould dish decorated with trailed slip.
Child 16

Dishes made in a mould with applied and decorated rims. Child 16

a. Slip of a contrasting colour can be trailed directly on to the pot: it must be definite and bold and the pattern worked out beforehand. It can, in fact, be marked out on the surface with a fine point. The result stands out slightly and is raised above the surface. Names can successfully be applied in this manner and the only trap to avoid is giving the pot a Christmas-cake look.

b. The whole of the inside of the dish can be covered with slip and various treatments can be carried out on it.

Method

a. Ensure that the surfaces and edges are smooth and even; the dish must be in the mould and the slip applied while the clay is still soft.

b. The slip should be well mixed with no lumps or bits.

c. Pour sufficient slip in the dish to cover the inside—say, about half a cupful.

d. Hold the mould in both hands and tip it so that all the inside is covered.

e. Pour out the surplus slip but hold the dish firmly in the mould with the fingers on the rim, as the outside surface may have been dried out slightly by the plaster.

f. Rest the mould flat and with long strokes of a fine sponge, wipe away any slip from the edges or from the mould itself.

This slip surface can either be left as a contrasting colour or it can be decorated in a variety of ways:

1. Sgraffito. When the slip has lost its shine or become leather-hard, it can be either scratched, or cut to reveal the body underneath.

2. Slip Trailing. As well as being trailed on to the surface of the pot, slip can be trailed on to the wet surface of the slip. Another colour is used and the trailing can follow the traditional patterns such as feathering, or it can be an individual pattern or design. The slip is trailed carefully and takes on a smoother, less harsh quality than when it is trailed on to the surface of the clay itself.

However, if the results are disastrous, then there are two alternatives though one, strictly speaking, is the wrong way to go about making a design:

a. Wipe away all the slip with a sponge and make a new start. This can only be done once or twice as the clay becomes too wet and eventually may split.

b. A marbling effect can be obtained by carefully swishing the slips round inside the dish. Pleasant effects can often be obtained by this method. This is indeed, a very legitimate method of decorating, especially if the slips are carefully chosen from the start and the movement is carried out carefully.

3. Stencils can be cut out of newspaper and pressed on to the surface of the clay and then the inside can be slipped. As the slip dries, the paper comes away from the surface leaving a clear pattern. Wax resist can be used instead of paper. Only fairly small pieces of paper are effective, as the slip tends to creep under the edges of the larger pieces.

The edges of the dish can be left either straight and flat, decorated with an incised pattern, or rounded to remove the sharp edges. The rim is important though, and it must be left neat and tidy all round whether it is decorated or left plain.

Mould pots decorated with slip can be glazed with a transparent glaze on the inside only to great effect, especially if red clay has been used for the body. The dark red roughness of the unglazed body contrasts pleasantly with the shiny decorated interior. However, for more functional ware, it is often desirable to glaze the outside too.

Dishes which have not been decorated while the clay is still wet can be painted in underglaze colours after being biscuit fired. These methods are described in Chapter 7.

Mould dish with oxide decoration. Child 16

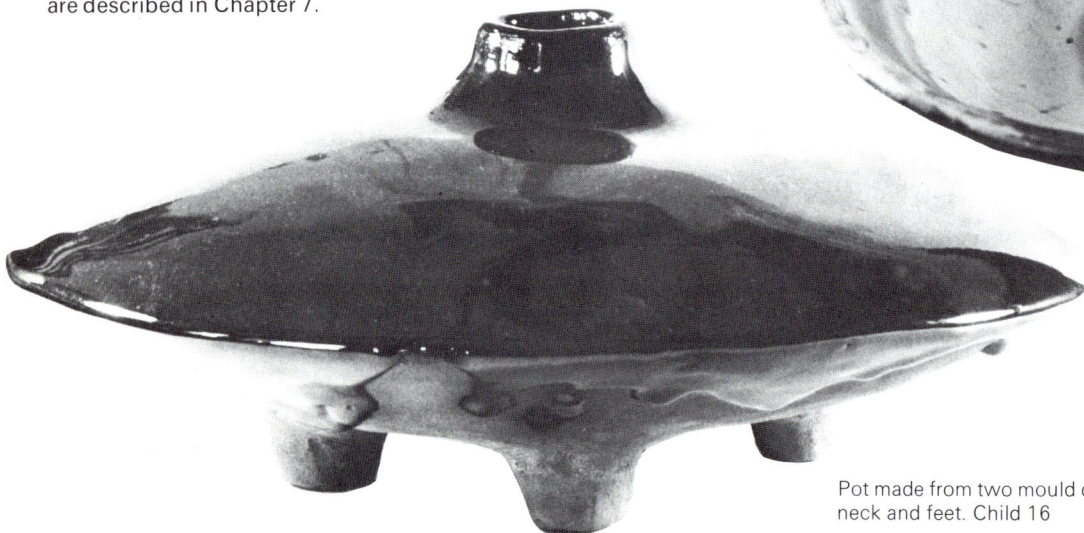

Pot made from two mould dishes with applied neck and feet. Child 16

clay

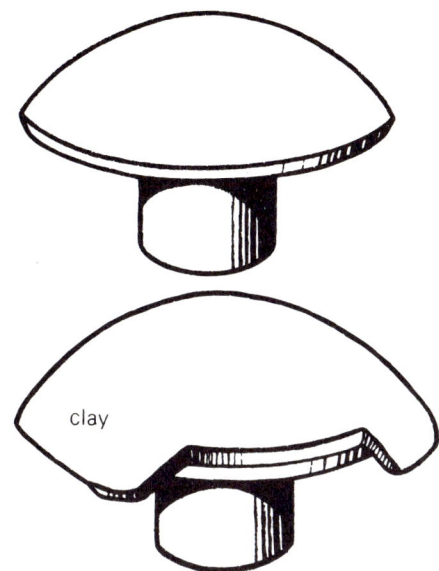

Hump or mushroom mould

This is another variation on the single-piece mould and is generally based on a circle. The mould is made rather like a mushroom and clay is draped over it. The advantages of this mould are that complicated slip trailing can be carried out on a flat clay surface which is allowed to harden slightly before being put over the mould, without the pattern being spoilt; the pots can also be made quite quickly on this mould and various methods of decoration attempted, although it is unwise to attempt to slip the inside of these dishes as they often soften and collapse as the water is absorbed.

The mould is made in a similar way to the press-in type, although if the model is round it can be turned even on a wheel. Again, there must be no sharp corners or any under-cutting which would prevent the dish leaving the mould. The main difference is that in this case the actual pot is larger than the model, as it takes the internal measurements, while with a press-in dish, the model shows the external dimensions. It is possible, of course, to make a hump mould from a press-in mould:

a. the model is made,

b. a press-in mould is made from the model,

c a hump is made from the press-in mould.

If the press-in mould is not wanted, this is called a waste mould. It is important to prevent the plaster sticking together when one mould is being made from another. This is done by blocking the surface of the plaster with a weak mixture of soft soap and water. This should be applied to the surface several times, and allowed to dry in between applications. Surplus mixture should be removed and the surface of the plaster will eventually become quite waterproof and shiny. Petroleum jelly does work, but often leaves a rough surface.

The stalk of the mushroom should be fixed while the mould is being made and can be done by pushing a cardboard tube into the plaster of the mould before it has hardened and then filled up with more plaster. The thicker the stalk, the more stable the mould will be.

Hump moulds can also be made in clay and fired to low biscuit temperature, at which the clay will remain fairly absorbent. They are normally thrown upside down and the surface of the mould part is turned later. These are more hard-wearing than the plaster ones, more pleasant to use and on the whole more satisfactory.

Hump moulds are covered in a similar way to press-in moulds. The clay is rolled out and, if it is not to be decorated at this stage, it is patted over the mould, first with the hands and then with a damp sponge. The edges of the dish are trimmed with a wire cutter and can be cut flat or at an angle; again the edge needs to be of even thickness all the way round and as neat as possible.

The main advantage of this type of mould is speed and a chance to decorate a flat slab of clay with a pattern which would be impossible once the dish was made. Positioning a slab of clay which has been decorated by the traditional method of feathering presents no problems, but if a design has a centre, then care must be taken when it is dropped over the mould.

These dishes can be glazed like the pressed-in dishes—either all over or on the inside only.

This chapter has dealt with the making of pots from plaster moulds. There is another use of plaster and clay which, while being of interest to the sculptor rather than the potter, is still a fascinating technique.

Into a block of fairly soft clay, tools of various sizes and shapes are pressed. An incised pattern is made in the clay. A plaster cast of this is now taken and, when the plaster has hardened, the clay is gently removed. It is worth noting that plaster should not be poured on to really soft clay, or an unpleasant, rough surface will result. Any under-cutting does not matter: the clay can gently be picked out, as the plaster slab is the finished object. Many natural objects can be pressed into the clay and their natural texture will be recorded: rope, string, scissors, tools, saws, nails, shells will all work well.

The method is very simple; the actual making of the pattern is the most exciting and creative part, which is as it should be for something of this nature. The plaster can be treated in many ways, either with water colour or any other form of paint or polish.

6 Wheel pottery

Throwing pots on the potter's wheel is the most difficult technique in pottery to describe with words. It is a tactile process which demands a high co-ordination between brain and body. Only when the clay is fully under control can competence as a thrower be claimed and this requires considerable and regular practice over a long period of time.

There are many potters whose main concern is with hand-built pots and who think of throwing as something more mechanical; they think the hand-building techniques allow more opportunity and time for the consideration of shapes, development of form and texture, none of which is possible with throwing. Again, because of their very nature, thrown pots are based on the circle and only by carving or tapping can they deviate from it. However, for all this, the wheel still has a fascination which cannot be denied, and it is only when the skill has been mastered that many potters leave it, often returning to hand-building techniques. The feel of the wet clay between the hands, the control of the spinning pot and, with a kick wheel, the intimate satisfaction of machine, material and mind fully integrated, are experiences which give intense pleasure.

Equipment

1. The use of the wheel in pottery has been known to man for thousands of years. There are drawings showing the Egyptians using it in 5000 BC, while in China it dates back to at least 1000 BC. In principle, all the wheels are similar; the clay revolves while the hands remain still. The wheel-head which revolves the clay is moved by a much larger and heavier wheel known as the fly-wheel, which is either kicked or pushed round. Today this force may come from an electric motor instead of directly from the thrower.

A good wheel is essential. Experienced craftsmen find it difficult, if not impossible, to work on some modern wheels which are badly designed and cheaply made yet are expected to be quite sufficient for the beginner, who needs all the help that equipment can give him. Electric wheels are excellent for the beginner, as concentration can be centred on the clay and need not be divided between kicking and controlling the clay. Unfortunately they are so expensive that the price is often prohibitive. Many manufacturers make electric wheels, and a fuller survey of them can be found in Chapter 9, but the main requirement of an electric wheel, apart from its safety, is that it must be capable of running at a low speed, of about 30–40 revolutions per minute.

A kick wheel allows more direct control of the throwing process, with no machine intervening, but the thrower does need to be sitting while working so that a good, steady, even balance can be maintained. The Leach wheels and the more expensive Wenger wheels are both excellent. If a wheel which requires the thrower to stand is available, two students can work together, taking it in turns to kick and throw.

2. The clay must be well prepared and be on the soft rather than the hard side, especially for beginners. A 'tight' clay is not so suitable as one which is more open and moves more easily. As with a wheel, poor throwing clay is as impossible for the experienced craftsman to control as for the student; with practice good clay will easily be recognized.

Cinerary urn. Thrown pot decorated with a face. Roman, first century AD

Corean pot, thrown and carved. Seventeenth or eighteenth century

Round lumps, about 1½ or 2 lb in weight are admirable for practice. Clay can be made more open by the addition of a small percentage of sand.

3. The amount of other equipment required is fairly small but important, and should be to hand before throwing starts (tools need to be clean):

a. Bowl of clean water, large enough for the hand.

b. Single and double (twisted) wire.

c. Small fine natural sponge (the elephant-ear shape is very good).

d. Wooden tool for trimming base.

e. Sponge on the end of a stick for mopping out the inside of tall pots.

f. Needle in the end of a cork.

g. Board or tile for finished pots.

Theory and practice

The theory behind throwing is that the centrifugal force exerted by the revolving wheel, combined with pressure from the hands, forces the clay to be built upwards rather than to spread outwards, which it undoubtedly would if it were allowed. Before a pot can be built up the clay must be perfectly central on the wheel, otherwise a lopsided pot will result, which may eventually collapse. When a pot goes off centre it is much better to start the whole process again rather than to try to put it back on centre, which is difficult even with experience. In practice, the pot is built up in the following way:

1 Centring the clay

Method

a. A good speed is built up (anti-clockwise). (Electric wheels three-quarter to full speed.)

b. Clay is thrown on to the dry wheelhead with a sharp movement.

c. Elbows rest against the side of the body, forearms rest if possible, on the edge of the wheel trough, both hands round the clay gently exerting pressure. Water should be used as a lubricant to prevent the clay sticking to the hands and to make movement easier. More water is required as the clay goes dry. The pressure should come from the palms of the hands rather than the fingers and should be firm without being hard. On no account should the hands be allowed to wobble nor should the clay be controlling the hands. Gentle pressure should cause the clay to go upwards and form a cone.

d. The pressure should be relaxed yet firm: rather like that of a wrestler who uses his knowledge and experience to put pressure in the right place.

e. The cone can now be pressed downwards with the thumbs over the top and the hands at the side; on large lumps the cone can be pressed down with the right palm while the left hand controls the clay as it comes down.

f. These movements need to be repeated two or three times until the clay is centred and is going round completely evenly. With experience the feel of the clay will tell the thrower when this has been achieved; but centred clay looks as if it is still, while in fact, it is rotating.

g. Hands or fingers should always be taken away from the clay gently, or wobbling will occur if the pressure is relaxed suddenly. It is quite hope-

For illustration see photographic action sequence 1

less to go beyond this stage before centring is mastered. Pots cannot be made from unevenly centred clay by anyone, and although the natural temptation is to want to run on ahead and make pots, it is unwise to do so; it is only confusing to the student to be shown a whole series of processes, when only one can be tackled at a time.

2 Opening out

This can only take place when the clay has been successfully centred. The process is similar to the one described in Chapter 3, for the opening out of thumb pots. In principle the thumb has to be driven down the centre of the clay and the base of the pot formed.

Method

a. Medium wheel speed.

b. The left elbow is tucked into the side, the forearm resting on the trough and the hand round the clay, with the thumb over the top.

c. The right hand is over the clay with the fingers resting on the left hand for support; the thumb is kept as straight as possible, and pushed slowly down the centre of the clay to within $\frac{3}{4}$" of the wheelhead. This allows for a fairly thick base.

d. The thumb now makes a swinging out movement which forms the inside of the base: the potter has his pot in mind by this time, and this movement should establish the design of the pot.

This opening out stage, too, is very important, because until it is mastered, no pot can be made. It is a good idea to think of it, at the beginning, as an end in itself, and practise it until the clay has been opened out perfectly evenly and smoothly.

3 Throwing

This is the process of bringing the clay up from the lump at the base to form the walls of the pot and can only be carried out successfully when the clay has been centred and opened out evenly. A cylinder is a good shape to aim for in the first place, as it does not raise the question of good or bad design; besides which it is a very good exercise.

The elbows are tucked into the side as often as it is convenient throughout the whole throwing process—this helps to prevent wobbling. It is up to the individual student to work out a comfortable and relaxed position suitable to him. The throwing takes place on the radius of the circle of the pot and the pressure must always be on this radius otherwise the pot will go off centre. The wheel speed is much lower at this stage— quarter speed for an electric wheel is usual, though large pots need a slower speed than small ones. The movements of the clay and the fingers must be allowed to follow the speed of the wheel, as too rapid movements will cause the pot to develop a thick spiral of throwing lines which are often difficult if not impossible to remove.

Method

a. Steady, slow speed.

b. The left hand goes inside the pot and the index finger is used for throwing; the index finger of the right hand, bent round slightly, goes outside; on small pots the thumb of the left hand can touch the right hand and this helps to establish contact between the two hands and makes the process easier.

c. The outside finger needs to be slightly lower than the inside one, and

For illustration see photographic action sequence 2

gentle pressure at the base will cause a roll of clay to be formed and this should be gradually brought up the pot by these two fingers.

d. The fingers must move up the pot gradually and the pressure must be released gently at the rim.

e. On no account should the rim be allowed to get thin or the pot may split, apart from making it look very weak. It needs to be kept thicker rather than thinner, especially if some sort of neck or special rim is required. A thicker rim also helps to prevent the pot from being forced outwards by centrifugal force.

f. This process should be repeated until the clay has been extended as far as possible. The walls need to be of even thickness except at the base, which should be slightly thicker to support the upper walls.

g. The rim can be smoothed off with the fingers of the left hand support- ing the walls and the right index finger resting on top. A good rim for mugs and drinking vessels can be obtained by using a strip of chamois leather wrapped over the rim. As a guide, drinking vessels need a rim which slopes outwards slightly to be comfortable.

h. Water which collects in the bottom of the pot needs to be removed from time to time with the sponge while the wheel is spinning. In fact, the pot should only be touched while it is spinning, until completed.

i. *Collaring* may be necessary if the walls of the cylinder tend to go out- wards or get forced out by the hand. Both hands are moistened, wrap- ped gently round the lower part of the pot and are brought slowly up it, gradually drawing in the walls. The process is a gentle one, and may need to be repeated two or three times before the walls are straight.

j. *Trimming* the top of the pot will be necessary if it is uneven. It can either be done with a sharp point, such as a needle stuck into a cork or with a fine wire held at right angles to the wall of the pot on a radius of the circle. Pots thrown on centre rarely need trimming and if one side persists in growing more than the other, it is probably because the opening out process was not carried out evenly.

k. When the pot has been thrown and the inside dried out, the surplus clay can be removed from the wheelhead and the base of the pot, and it is ready to be removed from the wheel. Any measurements required should be taken before it is removed and any distortion takes place.

Removing pots from the wheel

There are three methods which can be used, each one having its own advantages.

1 Sliding

Method

a. The base of the pot is tidied up with a wooden tool, the wheel stopped, and flooded with clean water.

b. A thin single wire is passed underneath the pot and is pushed as near to the wheelhead as possible, so that the minimum amount of clay is left. This is repeated and if necessary more water may be flooded on to the wheel. The pot should now be separated from the wheel with a thin layer of water.

c. A tile or a flat piece of wood or asbestos is flooded with water and held at the edge of the wheelhead to receive the pot.

For illustration see photographic action sequences 4 and 5

d. The pot is now pressed at the bottom by the thumb, middle and index finger of both hands; the pressure needs to be at the base of the pot and should be gentle but firm: the pot should slide gently across the wheelhead and on to the tile at the side.

The disadvantages of this method are:

1. Damage may be done to the pot by pressing it.
2. Each pot needs an individual board—therefore more space needed.
3. It is not possible with large or tall pots.
4. The pots always need to be turned.
5. The pots may crack across the base if thin, due to the water.

The advantages are:

1. A good method for a small pot, and pots which have narrow bases and need turning.
2. Good for beginners.

2 Lifting

Lifting pots from the wheel is a much faster technique but requires more skill.

Method

a. The pots need to be thrown fairly quickly and as little water as possible should be used. The outside walls need to be gently scraped with a wooden tool in the final process to remove any slurry and give a dry surface. The base of the pot should also be carefully cleaned, with a crisp finish and a slight undercut on the base gives a springing look.
b. A twisted wire is passed underneath the pot while the wheel is gently spinning. One revolution of the wheel is normally sufficient, though potters tend to develop their own method. The twisted wire should leave a neat line pattern on the base besides pulling in air.
c. Both hands, clean and dry, need to be used to lift the pot from the wheel. They should grip the pot as near to the base as possible and lift gently—more from one side to begin with, then the other. The base of the pot ought to be left fairly thick for this reason. With taller pots, a piece of newspaper can be gently attached across the rim while the wheel is in motion; this will help it to keep its shape while being lifted. The pot should be put down on to a clean dry surface.
d. Pots which have been lifted off the wheel need little or no turning; this is a further development of throwing technique which requires the pot to be thrown quickly and conceived in its entirety while being thrown.

The main advantages of this method are:

1. Speed.
2. Little or no turning.

3 Lifting with a scraper

This is a very quick method and useful for small pots. Paint scrapers work very well.

Method

a. The method described in No. 2 above is followed as far as the twisted wire is pulled under the pot. Then the wheel is stopped.
b. A wet, clean scraper is gently eased underneath the pot after the wire has been used.
c. The pot is now lifted, put down carefully and the scraper removed.

For illustration see photographic action sequences 6 and 7

d. These pots will need to be turned but it is a very good method for saucers, fairly flat wide based pots and small pots generally.

4 Working on a batt

Many pots, because of their very nature, cannot be either lifted or pushed from the wheelhead, so they have to be made on a board or a batt, rather like an artificial wheelhead, which can be lifted instead of the pot. Large plates, bowls, tall pots for instance, are always made on batts, which can be made from asbestos, thick hardboard or plywood.

Method

a. A lump of soft clay is centred and flattened on to the wheel to a thickness of about $\frac{1}{2}$"–$\frac{3}{4}$".

b. This is deeply scored with concentric circles and finally a tool is used to make a cross.

c. The dampened batt is pressed on to this, and a swift tap in the middle will keep it in position.

d. Throwing now continues normally, but care must be taken to make the first movement one which presses the clay down on to the batt and thus helps to make the batt sit firmly on the clay.

e. After the pot has been made, it should be cut underneath, to allow it to contract without sticking to the batt or splitting. Besides which, it is extremely difficult to cut under a leather-hard pot on a batt. The batt is gently prised off the clay and the whole removed. The clay chuck can be used many times if it is checked to ensure it is still flat.

So far the throwing of a cylinder has been dealt with: this is an excellent exercise as the cylinder forms the basis of all shapes other than plates and bowls. It needs to be practised frequently until competence can be claimed, and then the other basic wide shapes, such as a bowl, can be tried.

Bowls

Bowls are not made by quite the same method as cylindrical or tall pots. The clay needs to be fairly soft, and medium or large bowls need to be thrown on a batt to prevent them collapsing while being removed from the wheel.

Centring takes place in the same way but the centred clay should be flatter rather than taller, and the diameter will determine the maximum width of the bowl. The opening out process is very different and needs careful attention.

Method

a. The clay is centred but is left flat.

b. To open out the bowl, the hands can be held in the same way as described earlier.

c. The thumb goes down the centre of the clay and the top of it opened out rather in the shape of an inverted cone; there is no swinging out movement as the inside of the bowl must be without angles.

d. The walls are pulled up gradually without being allowed to open out. They need to be fairly thick to allow the bowl later to be opened out.

e. As the final process, the bowl can be gradually opened out; as a guide, the top diameter cannot be more than twice that of the base. Out-

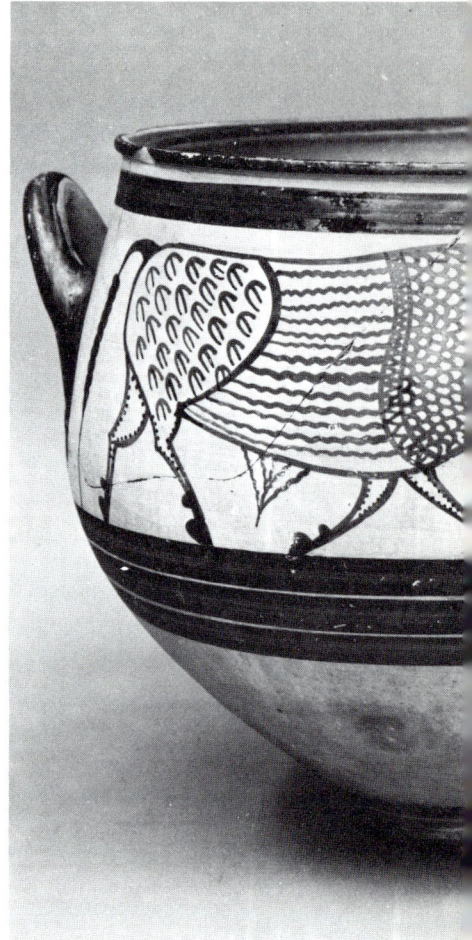

Open bowl or krater with brushwork animals. Mycenaean

For illustration see photographic action sequences **10** and **9**

ward-going rims are much more difficult to control than ones which point inwards as they tend to split and collapse more easily.

f. The interior profile should be smooth, even and continuous, with no ridges or bumps.

g. The clay left at the base is removed while turning and the external and internal profiles must be as closely integrated as possible during all stages.

Turning

Pots which have been thrown on the wheel generally need finishing on the base. Surplus clay is removed and a good crisp foot is made which can change the whole character of the pot. Some potters regard turning as an unnecessary mechanical process which should be avoided or kept to a minimum; while at the other extreme some potters think turning is a vital part in the manufacture of a pot, and if necessary the whole of the walls must be turned. There is, however, a happy medium: the pot is conceived as a whole while it is being thrown and turning is the final process which reveals the shape. It is a functional process and also one which can impose its own character. Turning tends to give a crisp, definite, clean and fine quality, which can give a bowl, or any pot for that matter, an individual quality.

Method

a. The pot is allowed to dry slowly and evenly until it is leather- or cheese-hard, that is, it will support its own weight, can be lifted without warping, yet is still slightly pliable. Many pots dry more evenly if they are turned upside down when strong enough. This is especially so with bowls.

b. It is centred upside down on the wheel and held in position by lumps or rolls of clay. The centring can be assisted by following the lines on the wheelhead or marking them on in pencil. Otherwise it can be done by tapping the pot to the centre as the wheel spins slowly or by allowing the wheel to revolve, holding a finger or tool against the wall to make a mark to show where it is off centre, and then gently pushing the pot into the correct position. This last method is rather a slow one, but it does work until the hand and eye are co-ordinated sufficiently to use the tapping method.

   For repetition throwing, a chuck can be turned in clay on which the pots will sit; this is especially useful, if not essential, for plates, though this technique really applies to the more advanced craftsman.

c. The actual turning is similar to the method a carpenter uses on his lathe. A metal tool with a fairly sharp edge is required, which can be made from banding wire or purchased as such from a supplier. The tool is held at an angle of about 60° to the pot, which needs to be spinning fairly quickly. The outside of the pot is turned first, and the foot and the centre left until last. The tool must be held firmly and not allowed to wobble. Both hands can be used and the elbows pressed into the sides if possible. Clay should come away cleanly and not stick to the body. If it does, then the pot is probably too soft, and should be allowed to harden slightly. Any wobbling or rippling on the pot surface probably means the clay is too soft. Turning removes

For illustration see photographic action sequences **11** and **12**

surplus clay and the finished pot should be the same thickness throughout. Bowls particularly are enhanced by turning, which gives them a spring, as it removes the surplus clay. The foot must be considered in relation to the rest of the bowl, and it can give it the growing look which most good bowls possess. As a guide, the foot of the bowl should be no more than one-third of the diameter of the rim.

Handles

Handles should be a reflection of the method by which a pot is made. A thrown pot needs one which has been pulled, a coil pot should have a rolled handle, and so on. Naturally, this is a guide rather than a law, as exciting results can be obtained from the use of different methods on the same pot.

Pulled handles are made from a rectangular lump of clay which is gently stroked at one end with the thumb and fingers of the right hand, using plenty of water as a lubricant. The handles should be thicker at the top end, i.e. the end which is to be joined to the pot. A cross section of a handle should show a slightly flattened oval rather than a strap-like section. After it has been pulled it should be nipped off with the end of the thumb and laid on a wooden surface to harden slightly before being put on to the pot.

Method

1. A lump of well kneaded, rather stiff clay is cut into blocks about 6" long, 1" wide and ½" thick.
2. Hold the lump of clay vertically in the left hand in front of the face so that the movement of the fingers can be carefully watched and controlled.
3. Using the right hand, well lubricated with water, stroke the clay downwards to form the handle.
4. Keep the top end of the handle slightly thicker to enable it to be well joined on the pot.
5. When the shape has been formed nip off the handle sharply with the end of the thumb and lie it on a wooden board to harden slightly before fixing to the pot.
6. Several handles can be pulled from the same lump of clay.

A variation of this method is to pull each handle on a separate piece of clay, pull it over on to itself, and allow it to harden slightly, more or less in the shape it is to be on the pot.

Handles cut with a wire have a much sharper and cleaner appearance and were used extensively on cream pierced ware during the eighteenth century, and suit finely turned or moulded ware. A template or model is made in wire and this is pulled through a piece of prepared clay, the resulting handle being the same thickness at both ends; again, allow to harden slightly before fixing.

Fixing on the handles

1. The pot should be in a finished, leather-hard state. Handles should be dry enough to bear their own weight without bending.
2. The parts to be joined together should be scratched and painted with slip.
3. The top join is made first, the thickest part of the handle is pushed on

a Wire model for handle

b Wire pulled through clay

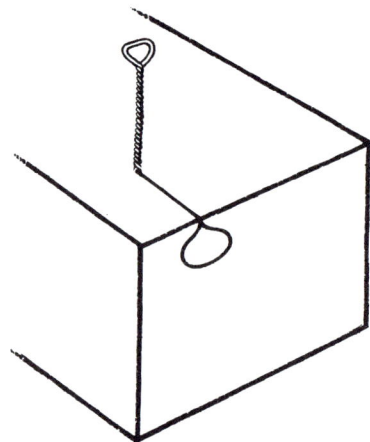

c Handle hardening

For illustration see photographic action sequence 13

to the pot and the join smoothed over with the thumb of the right hand, while the fingers support the rest of the handle.

4. The pot is now held horizontally, and, with a wet hand, the handle can be pulled smooth again.
5. The base of the handle is now fixed to the pot with a swift decisive movement.

For the other types of handles, it is only necessary to cut off the surplus clay and fix the handle as described above.

Some potters like to pull the handles on the pot itself.

Method

1. A rectangular lump of clay is patted more or less to the shape of the handle.
2. The top end is fixed to the pot as described earlier.
3. The pot is held in the left hand and the handle gently pulled with the right hand as for a pulled handle.
4. The bottom is joined on to the pot, and the pot is left upside down to dry.

Reference should be made to photographs or, better still, actual pots, to see how potters have related the handle to the pot as a whole, and to see just how many methods there are of doing a simple task of this nature, and the possible variations in shape. Not only should the handle be considered, but also the shape it encloses in relationship to the pot.

Jugs

A lip is made on a jug when the pot has been made and is still on the wheel.

Method

1. The outside wall is supported by two fingers of the left hand.
2. The index finger of the right hand gently pulls out the lip.
3. When the pot has hardened slightly, this lip can be enlarged by gently pressing it further down with a moistened sponge or finger.
4. As a general guide, the lip should be made larger and bolder rather than smaller, as it tends to spring out slightly while drying and assume its original shape.
5. A clean sharp edge is required for good pouring without dribbling. A lip must act as a funnel, channelling the liquid.

In general on the appearance of jugs and lips these points should be noted:

a. Small lips tend to look mean and are rarely efficient, while larger ones can give a jug grace and character.
b. Jugs, especially those designed for milk, need fairly large, open tops to allow for easy cleaning. The handle, too, should not come above the level of the rim or it will make it unsteady when upside down on the draining board.

Only the basic movements and techniques of throwing, turning, handling and making lips for pouring have been described here. More advanced techniques such as the joining of thrown parts together, as in a teapot, are beyond the scope of this book. Competent cylinders, bowls and jugs are no mean achievement, and form a sound basis for more advanced techniques.

56

1 Centring the clay

A good speed is built up (anticlockwise –electric wheels three quarters to full speed); clay is thrown on to the dry wheelhead with a sharp movement

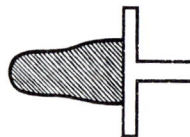

Elbows rest against the side of the body, forearms rest on the edge of the wheel trough, both hands round the clay gently exerting pressure. Water should be used as a lubricant to prevent the clay sticking to the hands and to make the movement easier. More water is required as the clay goes dry

The pressure should come from the palms of the hands rather then the fingers, and should be firm without being hard. On no account should the hands be allowed to wobble, nor should the clay be controlling the hands. Gentle pressure should cause the clay to go upwards and form a cone

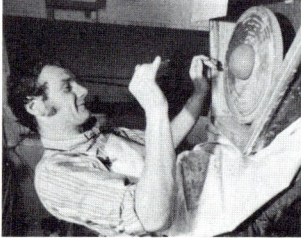

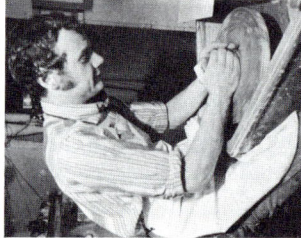

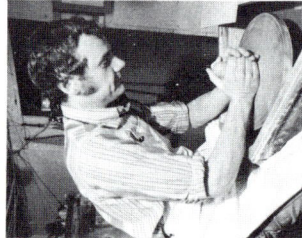

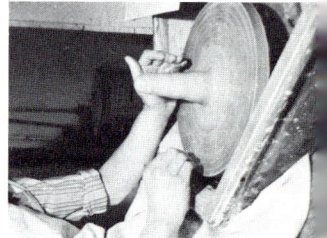

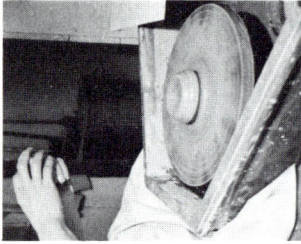

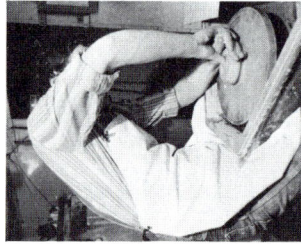

2 Opening out

The clay is now centred and ready for opening out

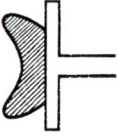

Medium wheel speed. The right hand is placed over the clay with the fingers resting on the left hand for support; the thumb is kept as straight as possible, and pushed slowly down into the centre of the clay to within $\frac{3}{4}$" of the wheelhead. This leaves a fairly thick base

The thumb now makes a swinging out movement which forms the inside of the base. This should establish the design of the pot, which the potter now has in mind

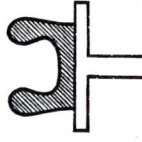

3 Throwing up the walls

Steady slow speed. The left hand goes inside the pot and the index finger is used for throwing. The index finger of the right hand bent round slightly, goes outside. On small pots the thumb of the left hand can touch the right hand. Contact between the two hands makes the process easier

The outside finger should be slightly lower than the inside one. Gentle pressure at the base will cause a roll of clay to be formed and this should be gradually brought up the pot by the two fingers

The revolutions on the wheel should be followed so that the process is gradual. Pressure must be released gently at the rim

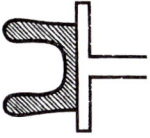

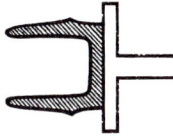

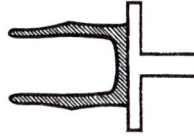

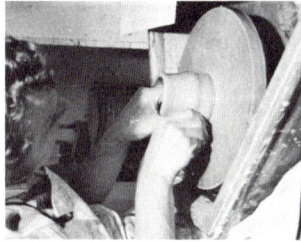

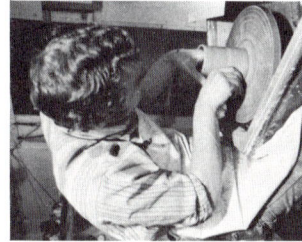

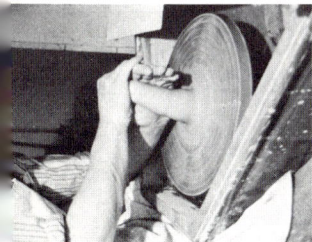

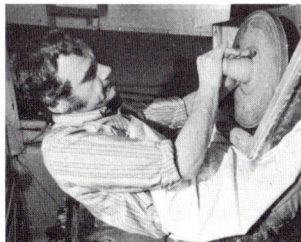

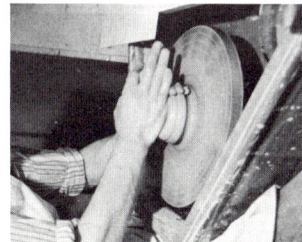

With large lumps, the cone of clay can be pressed down with the right palm while the left hand controls it

These movements should be repeated two or three times until the clay is centred and going round evenly

6 Removing pots from the wheel: sliding

The base of the pot is tidied with a wooden tool, the wheel stopped, and flooded with clean water

A thin single wire is passed underneath the pot and is pushed as near to the wheelhead as possible, so that the minimum amount of clay is left

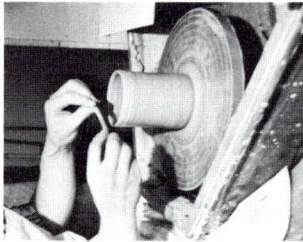

The pot is now pressed at the bottom by the thumb, middle and index finger of both hands. Pressure is exerted gently but firmly at the base of the pot

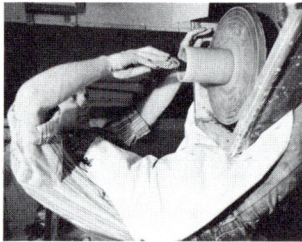

It should slide easily across the wheelhead and on to the batt at the side

4 Finishing off the pot on the wheel

The rim can be smoothed off, with the fingers of the left hand supporting the walls and the right index finger resting on top

A good rim for mugs and drinking vessels can be obtained by wrapping a strip of chamois leather round the rim. To be comfortable, drinking vessels need a rim which slopes outwards slightly

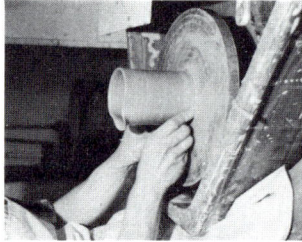

Water which collects in the bottom of the pot should be removed from time to time with a sponge while the wheel is spinning. In fact, until completed, the pot should only be touched while it is spinning

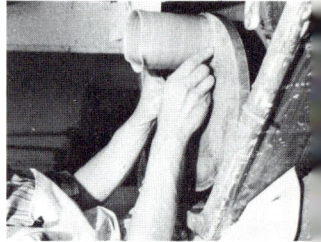

7 Removing pots from the wheel: lifting with a scraper

A twisted wire is pulled under the pot while the wheel is still revolving. No water is used

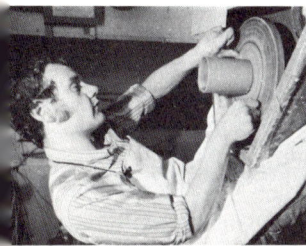

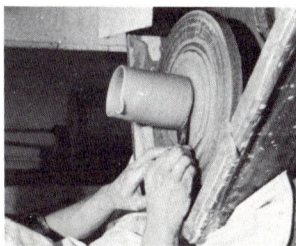

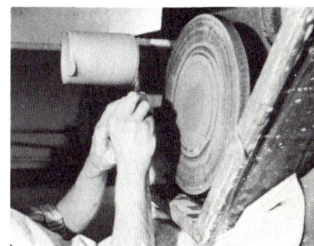

The wheel is stopped and a clean wet scraper is gently eased underneath the pot

The pot is now lifted, put down carefully and the scraper gently removed

5 Trimming

Trimming will be necessary if the top of the pot is uneven. A fine wire is held at right angles to the wall of the pot on a radius of the circle

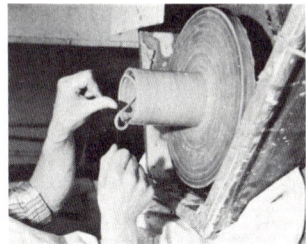

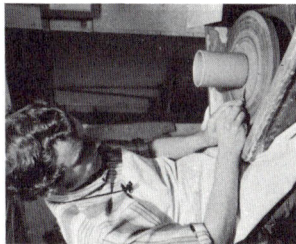

The surplus clay is lifted quickly from the pot with the wire

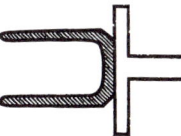

Surplus clay is wiped from the wheelhead and the base of the pot, which is now ready to be removed from the wheel. Notice that clay has been removed from the base. Any measurements required should be taken before it is removed in case distortion takes place

60

9 Bowls

The clay is centred but is left flatter than for a tall pot

The thumb goes down into the centre of the clay and pushes out the top leaving the bottom round and smooth. There is no swinging out movement as the inside of the bowl must be without corners

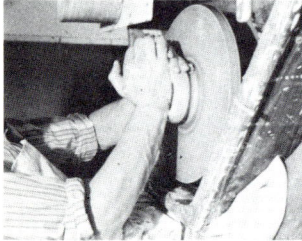

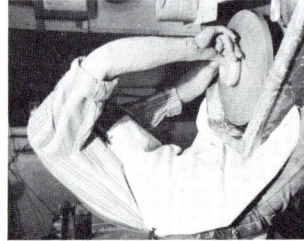

The walls are pulled gradually without being allowed to open out. For this reason they need to be fairly thick

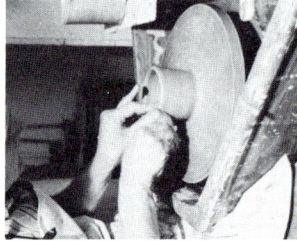

The bowl can be gradually opened out with increased pressure on the inside

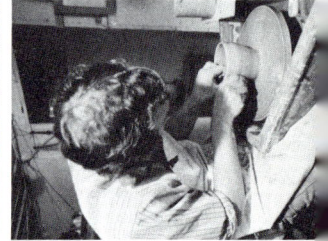

8 Jugs

The outside wall is supported by two fingers of the left hand

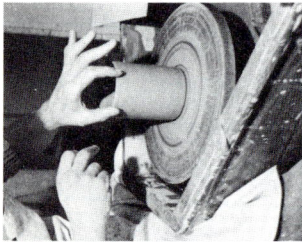

The index finger of the right hand gently pulls out the lip

A clean sharp edge is required for good pouring without dribbling. A lip must act as a funnel, channelling the liquid

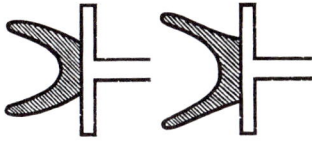

The final shape is approaching

The rim should be kept neat, rounded and full. It can be made thinner if necessary

The final shape: surplus clay is removed from the wheelhead with a wooden tool

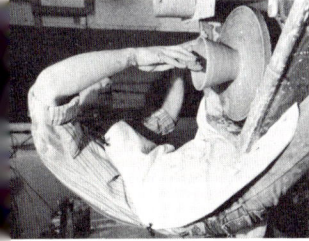

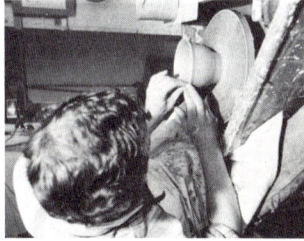

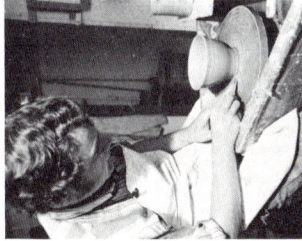

11 Turning

The pot is centred upside down on the wheel by tapping it towards the centre as the wheel spins slowly

It is held in position by lumps or rolls of clay pushed on to the wheelhead

Both hands are used and the elbows pressed into the sides to prevent wobbling. The turning tool is held at an angle of about 60° to the pot, which needs to be spinning fairly quickly

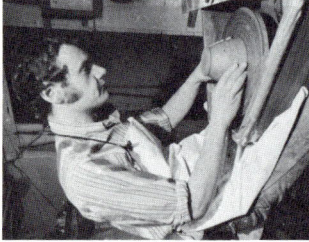

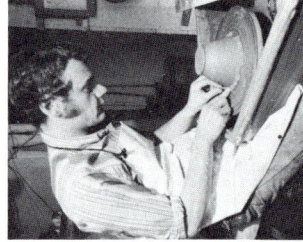

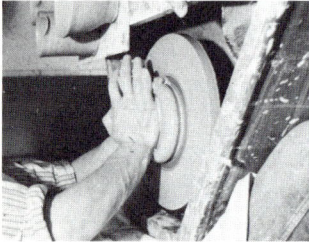

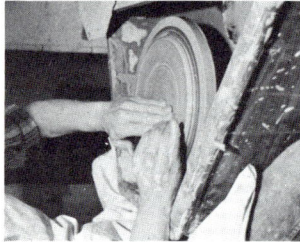

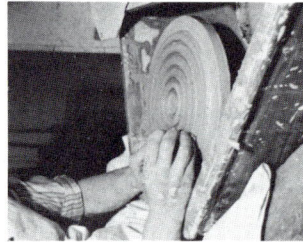

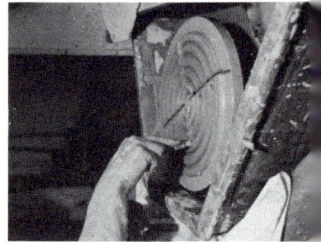

10 Working on a batt

A lump of soft clay is centred and flattened on to the wheel to a thickness of about $\frac{1}{2}"-\frac{3}{4}"$, using the side of the hand and . . . .

. . . then the fingers

A wooden tool is used to score deep concentric circles

A cross is made with this tool

The outside of the pot is turned first, the foot and centre left until last

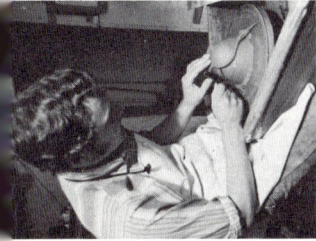

The foot is turned inside the base

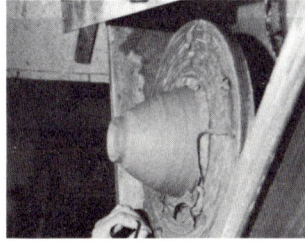

The finished bowl

The batt (in this photograph, asbestos) is moistened before being placed in position

The dampened batt is pressed on to the clay chuck

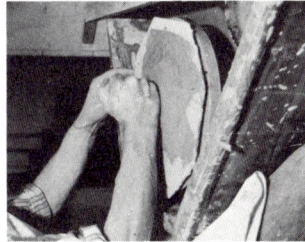

A swift tap in the middle of the batt will keep it in position

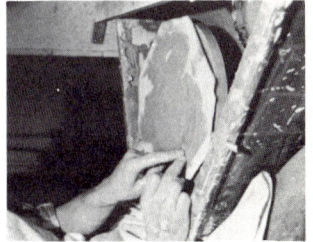

The batt is tested to see if it is level. Gentle taps can be used to correct it if necessary

13 Pulling handles (continued)

The top join is made first. The thickest part of the handle is pushed firmly on to the pot, and the join smoothed over with the thumb of the right hand, while the fingers support the rest of the handle

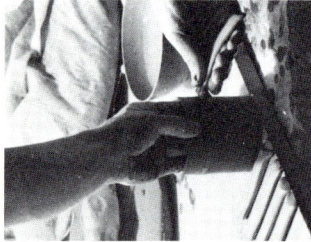

The left hand lifts the pot, and supports the handle so that underside can be smoothed

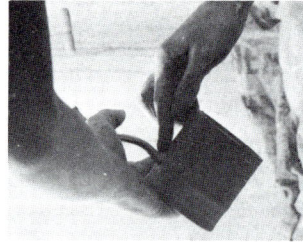

The pot is now held horizontally, and, with a wet hand, the handle is pulled smooth again

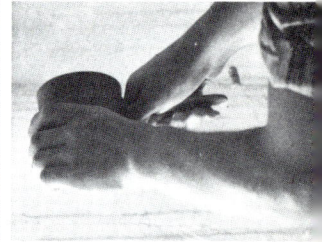

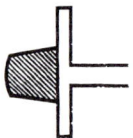

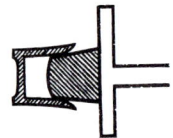

12 Turning on a chuck

A lump of fairly stiff clay is wedged and pushed into position on the wheelhead. The chuck is turned so that the sides are tapering only slightly

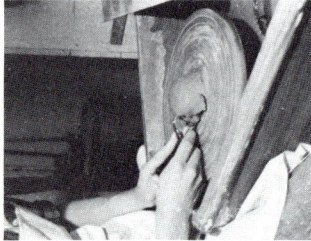

The pot is gently dropped into position while the wheel is spinning

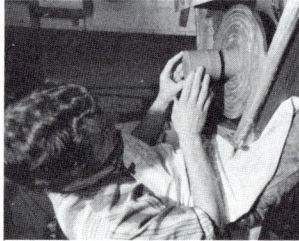

Now it is tapped until it revolves evenly

The pot is turned and removed from the chuck without stopping the wheel, by wrapping the hands round it

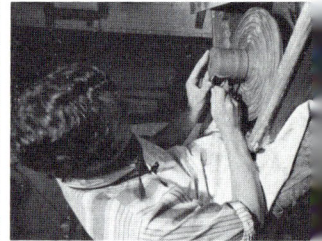

13 Pulling handles

The lump of clay is held vertically in the left hand in front of the face, so that the movement of the fingers can be carefully controlled

The right hand, well lubricated with water, strokes the clay downwards to form the handle. When the shape has been formed, the handle is nipped off sharply with the end of the thumb and slid on to a wooden board to harden slightly before being fixed to the pot

Handles lying on a wooden board to harden. The drawing shows the hardening handle viewed end-on

The pot is scratched and painted with slip while the handles are hardening

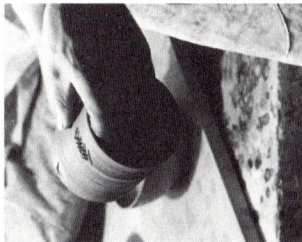

The handle is held between the thumb and first finger of the left hand, while it is tapped with the right hand to make it thicker and slightly rounded

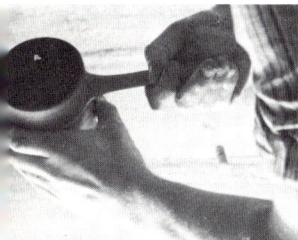

The front of the handle is smoothed

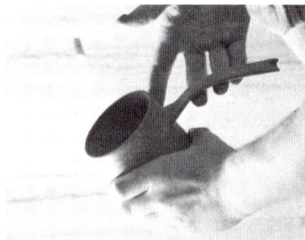

The handle should be supported while the pot is returned to the table

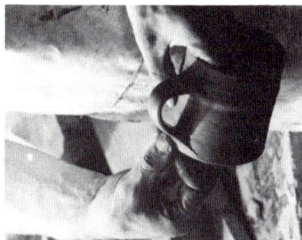

The base of the handle is fixed with a swift decisive movement

The finished mug

7 Glazing

When pots have been biscuit-fired (the first firing, changing the clay into pottery), they are usually covered with a glaze. This serves two purposes:

1. It makes them waterproof, and usually gives a smooth, practical, hygienic surface.
2. It is a method of adding colour and decoration.

Pots which are to be used on the table or to serve any practical purpose whatsoever usually have (1) as their priority, yet this often combines well with the decorative aspect, and both things have to be considered in relationship to each other, and to the pot.

Technical notes

Most of the materials used in pottery are more or less in their natural form and were, at some time, rock; most of them will melt to form a glass, if heated sufficiently, though this is not necessarily transparent. Clay itself will melt at a high temperature. Some materials, like feldspar, which is a combination of three different materials, will melt at the fairly low temperature of 1250°C. to form a simple glass. This, then, is how a glaze is formed. A substance which will melt to form a glass, often known as a 'glass-former', forms the basis of the glaze.

A 'glass-former' on its own is not practical from a potter's point of view. The purest and most widely used glass-former is silica, known to many as ordinary sand, or, in another form, flint or quartz; this melts at 1730°C. To bring this melting point to a more practical level, a flux is added. This causes the silica to melt at a much lower temperature. Lead is the main flux used in earthenware glazes; another flux in use at low temperature is borax. Fluxes such as calcium and magnesium, are used when a higher melting point is required, as for stoneware glazes.

Unfortunately, a glaze which consists only of silica and a flux tends to be unstable and often runs off the pot and so, to give the glaze body, another substance called alumina is added. This is as common as silica, but is rarely found in its pure state: usually it is combined with silica. It has a much higher melting point (2040°C.), which gives the glaze stability and increases its viscosity. It is combined with silica and water to form clay ($Al_2O_3 \cdot 2SiO_2 \cdot 2H_2O$). Thus, one atom of alumina is combined with two atoms of silica and two of water to form one molecule of clay.

This is a very simple introduction to the chemical background of glazes; as only earthenware glazes are being dealt with, the student who wishes to use stoneware glazes should refer to one of the books in the bibliography.

A glaze, then, is a combination of three parts—silica which gives the glass, alumina which gives the stability and depth, and a flux, which causes the whole to melt and form a glaze. Glaze materials rarely fulfil only one of these functions. Most are impure or are in combination.

A simple glaze was made by the mediaeval potters in England by dusting the damp surface of the pot with raw red lead or litharge. In the firing the lead caused the silica in the clay to melt on the surface of the pot to form a glaze. The glaze was not even, but this tended to add to the rugged strong quality of the work and added interest to the surface.

Today, lead is not used in its raw state as it is poisonous; the Department of Education and Science issued a Memorandum (No. 517) which laid down specifications for the types of lead which are permitted for use. These are explained more fully later. It is worth noting why lead is poisonous:

a. Once in the body it stays in the system and over a period of time large amounts can be built up.

b. As it is soluble in acid it is assimilated into the system through the acid in the stomach and can be absorbed through open wounds, i.e. cuts on fingers.

c. Some simple lead glazes used on pitchers in which any form of acid drink is stored such as lemonade, are dangerous, as lead from the glaze is quite likely to be dissolved by the acid in the liquid and is quickly absorbed into the system.

The lead-based glazes provided by pottery suppliers usually state that their glazes are made according to the specifications laid down by the Department and are, therefore, both safe to apply and to use. Usually the lead has been fritted (see below) with flint to make it insoluble both before and after firing. The silicates of lead—monosilicate, sesquisilicate and bisilicate—have approximately one part, one-and-a-half parts, and two parts of flint respectively to one part of lead, and while they are safe to handle it is as well to observe the following precautions:

1. Wash hands immediately after using glaze.

2. Never expose an open cut to glaze.

3. Never eat in a pottery, and wash hands thoroughly after completion of work.

A frit (from the French *frire*, to fry or to roast) is a mixture of materials heated until fusion takes place, and then ground down into powder. Some prepared glazes are frits, as are all the lead silicates. A simple transparent glaze can be made up from a mixture of:

5 parts by weight lead bisilicate
2 parts clay (this can be of the body of the pot)
It will mature about 1080°C./1100°C.

If red clay is used, the iron in the clay will cause the glaze to have a slight honey colour over a white body or slip which can give a warm and pleasant effect, found on much English slipware. A transparent glaze which is completely colourless can be made by either using white ball clay or china clay. The danger here is that this glaze may not fit over the body of the pot, and such faults as crazing may result; a remedy may be to substitute part of the clay used in the glaze recipe for part of the same clay as the body. Finding a glaze which is a good fit is often a slow business. These glaze faults are dealt with in a section later on in this chapter.

The simple glaze referred to above is known as a lead glaze as opposed to one actuated by an alkaline flux.

If a similar glaze is made by using 80 per cent borax frit and 20 per cent clay, the same colouring oxides added to the glaze will result in different colours. The chart on page 72 shows how they vary.

Educationally it is sound and desirable that children should know and have experience of all processes in pottery. Therefore they should know

Thrown and modelled salt cellar with salt glaze. English c 1744

what constitutes a glaze, and if possible have experience of mixing up a glaze and seeing how it works. However, it may be necessary for the teacher, especially when dealing with large numbers of children, to buy ready mixed glazes. This may sound like a heresy to some, but there is little joy in mixing up a whole batch of transparent glaze. But I think that as long as the teacher confines his buying of prepared glazes to the standard glazes, such as a transparent and opaque white glaze, this can be justified on two grounds, apart from convenience:

a. If they are supplied by the clay supplier they will have been designed to fit the body.

b. They can form the basis for experiments involving the addition of colouring oxides, and other materials.

One way of classifying glazes at earthenware temperature is into two types, transparent and opaque. A transparent glaze can be made opaque by the addition of 8 per cent to 10 per cent of tin oxide which suspends itself in the glaze and refracts the light. This glaze in fact forms the basis of the white majolica glazes of Spain and Italy, and was introduced into those countries by the invading Arabs. In Spain the resulting pots were known as Hispano-Moresque ware, typical of which was free lively brushwork, using lustres and colours, over the white glaze. The surface of the glaze is superb for majolica or underglaze painting, and the resulting brilliant yet slightly subdued colours should give it a permanent place in the school curriculum. Because the tin oxide is only suspended in the glaze, it must be applied as evenly as possible, as it gives the glaze a higher viscosity.

A transparent glaze is, perhaps, the most useful of all. It forms the base of many other glazes, and is ideal over slipware or, on a white body, with underglaze painting. It can be coloured easily with additions of oxides, and can take on the appearance of brilliant stained glass over white or coloured slips.

Glaze mixing

Glaze materials arrive in a dry, powdered state and can easily be weighed to the right proportions. All recipes in this book are given as parts by weight, i.e. grammes, ounces or pounds.

A glaze should be mixed carefully and a recipe followed, unless a note is made of any alteration, as nothing is more maddening than to get an exciting result without knowing how. For convenience and simplicity the total parts of a glaze should be as near to a hundred as possible. Recipes thus given can be quickly converted to any scale of weights employed and if oxides or other ingredients are added, they are usually added as a percentage over and above the whole. For instance, if the recipe of a glaze gave a total weight of 5 lb and it was decided to make an addition of 5 per cent iron, some calculations would have to be done:

5 lb = 80 ounces

5 per cent of 80

Formula

$$\frac{\text{Total Weight}}{\text{\% required}} \times 100 = \frac{80}{5} \times 100 = 4$$

Therefore 4 ounces of oxide would have to be added.

Dipping pot in glaze

Pouring glaze

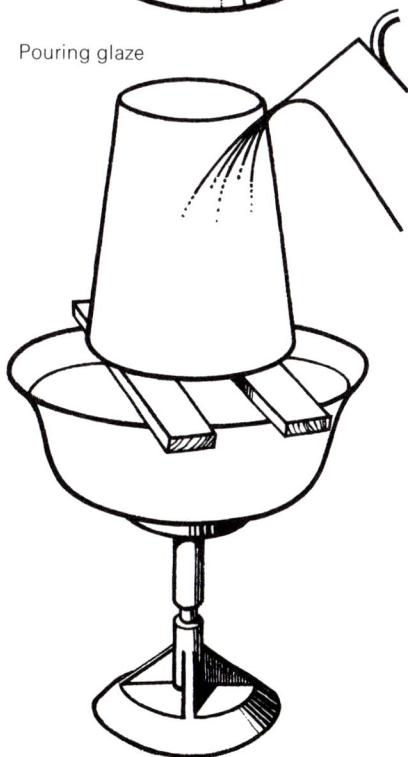

Once the amounts have been decided upon—and it takes about 5–7 lb. dry weight of glaze to fill a bucket—the ingredients can be weighed out. It is easier to add the dry materials to water rather than the other way about. The mixture must be stirred thoroughly with the hand, and any lumps broken up. This now needs to be put through a sieve—about 80 or 100 mesh will do—twice, or until all the lumps have disappeared and the glaze has an even consistency. If the glaze is too thin—usually it should be like single cream, though some glazes need to be applied more thickly—it should be allowed to settle, and surplus water removed from the top. A pot glazed too thinly will result in an unpleasant, dry, rough surface when fired and will be difficult to re-glaze. Incidentally, most raw materials, and oxides too, are either white or black in colour at this stage, so the colour of the raw glaze is no indication of the result.

Once a glaze has been decided upon, there is little virtue in mixing a small quantity. A bucket full of transparent and one of opaque glaze are useful, especially for larger pots, which can be dipped completely. All glazes must be stirred thoroughly before being used and be checked to ensure they are of the correct consistency. Glazes which contain a frit, such as a lead frit, tend to settle quickly, as they are heavier than the other materials, but an addition of 2 per cent of bentonite will help to correct this by causing it to remain suspended for longer periods.

Methods of glazing

There are several different methods which can be used, each one having its own advantages. Before glazing biscuit ware, make sure it is clean and free from dust, which if necessary can be removed with a stiffish brush. Handle the ware as little as possible to prevent grease marks which may prevent the glaze from sticking. Dust can cause the glaze to crawl during firing.

1 Dipping is the easiest method and probably gives the most even results. A large quantity of glaze is required and the pot should be put into the glaze sideways to prevent any airlocks. The pot may need to be left in the glaze for several seconds, depending on the thickness of the glaze. Generally the inside and outside can be glazed at the same time.

2 Pouring is good when pots are large or when there is only a small quantity of glaze. The pot can either be held by the foot over a bowl and the glaze poured on to it, or it can be supported on strips of wood over a bowl and then glazed. The inside should always be glazed first and if the walls of the pot are thin and become saturated with water, this must be allowed to dry out before the outside is glazed. The porous biscuit pot absorbs the water and causes the glaze material to remain on the surface. If the walls are already saturated then the glaze merely slides off. With pouring, it is much more difficult to get an even covering of glaze, though often this irregularity gives an added richness.

3 Spraying is mainly an industrial method and requires a considerable amount of equipment, such as a spraying booth and spraying equipment. While only small quantities of glaze are necessary and an even covering can be obtained, it is outside the scope of most schools, and should not be used unless all the correct equipment is available, as fine silica dust is dangerous if inhaled.

4 Painting and trailing. Painting glaze on to a pot rarely results in an even coating and consecutive brush strokes tend to remove the glaze applied with earlier ones; it is useful when only small selective areas have to be covered, such as on models or relief work. Glaze, like slip, can be trailed on to surfaces, though possibly it is most effective when used on flat surfaces such as tiles or low relief work. Patches of different coloured glazes can be separated and emphasised by trailing a black glaze between them, and a rich effect obtained.

When a pot has been glazed, the surface is very fragile and any accidental knocking of rims can result in the glaze falling off, and there-fore must be handled carefully, especially when being placed in the kiln. To ensure that the pot is properly glazed, the following points are useful:

1. Allow the glaze to dry before handling the pot.
2. Any patches which have been missed should be retouched with a loaded brush and thin patches painted over.
3. Obviously large blobs should be gently rubbed over with a finger.
4. Glaze on the foot and about $\frac{3}{8}''-\frac{1}{4}''$ up the side should be removed, either by scratching with a wooden tool, brushing with a stiff brush, or wiping over with a damp sponge. As glaze melts during the firing, any on the foot will cause it to stick to the kiln shelf and if the glaze runs at all, the clean rim round the base will help to prevent it from running on to the kiln shelf. An alternative method, used widely in industry, is to dip the entire pot and foot in glaze and stand it on spurs in the kiln. These are triangular-shaped supports made out of clay, with sharp points which support the pot, and actually stick to the glaze. After firing, the spurs are pulled off and the three small marks or blemishes can be smoothed down with a carborundum stone. The success of this method relies on:

a. The glaze being fairly thin and highly viscous.
b. The spurs having sharp points which are not worn or broken.
c. Careful placing in the kiln.

The advantages are:

a. The pot is covered with glaze all over and is thus waterproof.
b. The base is smooth with no rough unglazed foot.

The disadvantages:

a. The process is slightly longer, especially when a kiln is being packed.
b. If the glaze is not viscous, or is applied too thickly, it may run on to the spurs and attach it very securely to the pot.

It is advisable to have spurs available for special pots and for those pots being used to test a new glaze. If the pot is fettled in the ordinary way, with the glaze removed from the base and then stood on a spur, any running glaze will tend to stay on the pot and not run on to the kiln shelf.

It is much quicker and more expedient in school to use the fettling method (cleaning the foot), except when either the situation occurs as described above, or there is a special request for a particular piece of work to have a glazed foot.

Glaze spurs

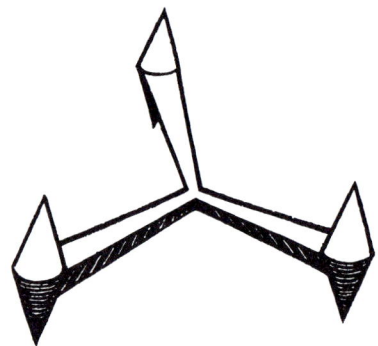

Colour in glazes

The colouring pigments used in pottery, either in glaze or painted on the surface, all derive from metal oxides. Generally the potter uses the common ones derived from iron, copper, cobalt and manganese, but rarer and much more expensive ones give the more uncommon colours.

Metal oxides vary in strength from oxide to oxide, and experiments need to be carried out to show the different effects.

Normally the oxides are prepared by the pottery supplier in a very finely ground powder form and can be added directly to the glaze, but some manufacturers stipulate their exact mode of use, recommending them, for instance, to be dissolved in boiling water or ground with a mortar and pestle, and any instructions given should be followed.

Common oxides

Cobalt oxide gives the blue known and used for many hundreds of years. It is available in different forms, perhaps the commonest being CoO. It looks black in its raw state and is strong in use. 0·125 per cent–2 per cent is usually sufficient to give a good colour. Sometimes the colour appears crude, especially when used in a white opaque glaze, and may need softening with 0·5 per cent of manganese or copper. It is the basis of the blue on Delftware and is perhaps the easiest colour in pottery to obtain, as it is active over the complete temperature range. Used in larger quantities it acts as a fairly strong flux, though this is not apparent when it is used in small quantities. It is very good in a transparent glaze over a white or blue slip or a white body. Sometimes it needs to be ground before use or it can cause speckles in the glaze. This effect may of course be desired. Its reaction depends upon the ingredients of the glaze, e.g., zinc oxide and leadless glaze causes it to be bright, while in lead glazes it tends to be inky.

Copper oxide gives a complete range of greens, black copper oxide CuO being the form in commonest use. The whole range of greens comes from copper; often they are soft and beautiful, sometimes hard, and any excess of copper will produce a crystalline, metallic black. Occasionally 0·5 per cent cobalt will help to stabilize the colour. Usually any amount from 1 per cent to 5 per cent will give sufficient colour. Copper gives different results in glazes with different fluxes. In a lead glaze, the colour is fairly bright and slightly lime; in an alkaline glaze where borax and soda have been used, the colour tends to be more turquoise.

Manganese oxide gives a range of browns, sometimes purple, and sometimes grey. Manganese dioxide (MnO_2) is used widely. The brown is not particularly attractive on its own, but with a small percentage of other oxides it does improve. It is often used for 'softening' the colours of the other oxides, and a small percentage in a transparent glaze helps it to flux and reduces the risk of it not fitting the pot.

Iron oxide is present in many clays especially red clay and to a lesser extent in ochre. The commonest form in use is Red Ferric Oxide (Fe_2O_3). In a transparent glaze, 1 per cent–5 per cent will give colours ranging from pale honey to treacle brown, and up to 4 per cent can be used in tin glazes.

Crocus martus is a natural form of iron which gives a red/brown colour when painted on to a tin glaze, though it does need to be applied in the correct thickness, which can only be discovered with practice.

All Oxides are intermixable and produce softer colours when more than one is used.

Oxide	Symbol	% required	Colour in Lead Glaze	Colour in Alkaline Glaze	Remarks
Iron Oxide	Fe_2O_3	1–10%	Honey to dark brown		
Manganese Oxide	MnO_2	2–9%	Browns	Purples	
Cobalt Oxide	CoO	0·25–2%	Blues	Blues	Very strong
Copper Oxide	CuO	1–6%	Greens	Turquoise	
Nickel Oxide	NiO	1–3%	Greys	Greys	Softens other colours in small percentages
Chromium Oxide	Cr_2O_3	1–4%	Matt greens	Greens	Gives red in low temperatures low alumina glaze
Vanadium Oxide	V_2O_3	2–10%	Yellows		
Rutile	TiO_2	1–5%	Yellow, mottled		
Tin Oxide	SnO_2	2–12%	White opaque	White opaque	Stiffens glazes
Zinc Oxide	ZnO	2–12%	White opaque		Small percentage brightens blues

Less common oxides

Chromium oxide (Cr_2O_3) is green in colour. It has a low solubility in glazes and when painted on to a tin glaze it gives a dark green opaque pigment, and forms the basis of most underglaze green pigments. However, when 2 per cent is used in a glaze with a very low alumina content, brilliant oranges and reds can result. The glaze is somewhat unstable, and is perhaps best used on flat surfaces. It must not be fired above cone 08 (940°C.), so it is suitable to be fired in a biscuit firing.

Vanadium oxide (V_2O_3) gives yellows. 2–10 per cent can be used.

Nickel oxide (NiO) will give grey when 1–3 per cent is used, and it is also very good for softening the colours of the other oxides.

Rutile is an ore containing titanium oxide and iron oxide. It gives a tan or brown colour in a glaze, but the titanium often affects the texture, giving a mottled, broken effect. Up to 5 per cent may be used.

Tin oxide or *Stannic oxide* (SnO_2) white in colour, renders transparent glazes opaque, and up to 10 per cent may be used. It remains in suspension in the glaze and therefore increases its viscosity.

Zinc oxide has a slightly opacifying effect and when very small quantities are used with cobalt, the resulting blue tends to be brighter. Zinc also acts as a flux in the higher temperature range, i.e. cone 1 (1100°C.) upwards, and is of little concern to the earthenware potter.

Various combinations of these oxides, when added to the basic glaze, can give a rich assortment of colours, and with carefully recorded and controlled experiments, a wide range can be built up. Trouble arises mainly when prepared pigments are used, and, often worse, prepared coloured glazes. The chance to achieve a special individual result has gone, and the resulting glazes are often crude in colour and have a smooth, industrial quality which renders them dull in comparison to the relatively simple but interesting home-made ones.

Underglaze painting

All the various oxides can be mixed with water, with perhaps a drop of glaze to keep them stable, and be painted on to the raw glaze. Naturally white opaque or pale light glazes show the colours off at their best; or the colours can be painted on to a transparent glaze over a white body.

Birds. Low relief decoration with painted oxides and transparent glaze. Children 14

Earthenware dish with a painted portrait of
King William. White tin glaze. Bristol, late
seventeenth century

As transparent glazes are more fluid, the colours tend to move and run
down the pot and so are unsuitable if a crisp clean design is required.

Majolica decoration consists of colouring pigments or oxides painted
on to the white tin glaze in its raw state. Because of the dry, powdery
surface of the glaze, the brush strokes need to be bold and free and the
design full and flowing. The pure white surface of the glaze almost
demands to be decorated and the colours take on a richness which is
luminous and fresh.

Prepared underglaze colours can be bought from pottery suppliers
and a wide range is available. However, all the oxides mentioned, with
the possible exception of chrome, can be used either alone or mixed
together, to produce a whole range of colours which are often more
interesting than the smooth, slightly mechanical quality which the bought
ones often have.

Method and points to note

1. Mix the colour with water either in a small basin, or on a plate or tile,
   or with a pestle and mortar where they can be ground for extra
   smoothness.
2. Use a soft brush with full bristles which come to a fine point, the fuller
   the better. Small brushes are of little or no use.
3. The raw glaze, when it is absolutely dry, is very absorbent, and the
   application of the colour may be difficult. Try painting on to the glaze
   before it has dried out completely. As far as possible use single brush
   strokes from a loaded brush.

4. If the pattern gets completely ruined, which is very rare, as accidental strokes and blobs can often be incorporated into the design, the whole glaze can be washed off, the pot dried out, re-glazed, and a fresh start made.

5. Before starting have an idea of the pattern, which needs to be as simple as possible. Practise beforehand on an old pot rather than a flat surface.

6. Banding the pot with lines is often a good beginning, as it establishes areas of pattern. Centre the pot on a free-spinning banding wheel, give the wheel a spin, and a loaded brush, lightly touching the side of the pot, will leave a clear straight line. Do the lines before the pattern, so they can act as a guide.

7. If ideas run out as far as pattern goes, it is useful to work out simple designs based on geometrical figures or letters of the alphabet. Lively patterns can result once work has started. This, of course, demands technical skill rather than artistic ability, but is quite legitimate when trying out a new medium.

A sample tile is useful for showing all the variations of colours and combinations available with a limited range of oxides. Each one must be clearly labelled and show the temperature at which it has been fired. A useful experiment showing the effect of a change of temperature is to make similar tiles fired to different temperatures, say 20°C. apart, and compare them. Holes made in the tiles when they are first made enable them to be displayed on the wall for permanent reference, where they can act as a stimulus for work or ideas.

Really clear designs can be obtained by firing the tin-glazed but un-painted pots to a low temperature—say 700°C.—at which the glaze hardens slightly and sticks to the pot, but is still porous. The design can then be painted on to the surface without any damage being done to the glaze, and the powdery surface is eliminated. The pot is fired again to the full temperature.

Pots which have been decorated need very careful handling to prevent the glaze from getting smudged or rubbed off. In a classroom this can be achieved by good planning; for example, a shelf near the kiln can be reserved for pots which have been decorated so that handling is restricted to the person packing the kiln.

On-glaze or enamel

This is a similar method of decoration to underglaze, but more sophisticated. Pigments or enamels, which are in fact carefully prepared low-temperature coloured glazes, and rather expensive, are purchased from the pottery suppliers. The lower the temperature, the easier it is to obtain bright colours. The higher the temperature, the more oxides giving colour burn out and disappear; generally speaking, at high stoneware temperatures (1250°C.) only the more natural colours are available. Enamels are painted on to a white tin glaze after the glaze firing; although white shows them up well, other light glazes can be used as a base.

Manufacturers usually supply their own instructions on how to use the enamels and these are usually on the following lines:

1. The powdered colour is mixed with a special oil-based medium pro-

Hispano-Moresque bowl. Painted lustre decoration. c fifteenth century

vided for the purpose on a tile. A palette knife is useful, saves wear on the brushes, and does mix the powder and medium well. Some manufacturers may recommend that the powder and medium be ground using a pestle and mortar. The mixture needs to be stiff but still quite fluid.

2. The design should be painted as firmly as possible, making sure that the enamel is applied fairly thickly and evenly. If necessary, the design can be repainted when dry. The medium suspends the enamel and makes it adhere to the surface of the pot.

3. Mistakes can be removed with turpentine and brushes must be cleaned fairly quickly to prevent them becoming hard.

4. The decorated pots need to be fired to a fairly low temperature, depending upon the colours used. About 750°C. (cone 016A) for most colours, but some may need a higher temperature. The kiln must be well ventilated to allow the evaporating oil to escape, or damage to elements may occur.

Lustres

These are similar to enamels. Their most extreme use can be seen in Victorian ware, where they were used to simulate objects made by quite different methods of manufacture, for example silversmithing. The Persians and Spaniards used lustres widely and freely. The lustres, like the enamels, are bought from the manufacturers, and are very expensive. They are ready mixed in liquid form and are used direct from the bottle. Interesting combinations of enamels and lustre can be made. Lustres can be painted successfully on to darker glazes. Brushes must be washed in methylated spirits, which can also be used to thin down the colour if necessary.

The lustres need to be fixed on to the pot in a low temperature firing (about 750°C.).

Wax resist

Just as this technique can be used for slip decoration, it is equally successful for resisting underglaze colours. Hot wax can be painted on to the raw glaze, and underglaze painted over the top. The wax resists the colour and the results can be very pleasant. Practice will show how the technique can be used to its best advantage. In double glazing (as described in the next section) effective use can be made of this method.

For special pots, the foot or base can be dipped in wax to prevent the glaze from adhering, thus fettling will be reduced to a minimum. If any wax is spilled on to the biscuit ware and needs to be removed, this can only be done satisfactorily by refiring the pot. Small areas can be rubbed with dry glaze, painted and the wax covered over.

Double or overglazing

One glaze over another can produce startling and exciting results, often richly textured. Double glazing is best used on small decorative pots rather than functional ware.

A coloured glaze is put on first and allowed to dry for a few minutes; a white or opaque glaze is then put over this. Coloured glazes, because of the presence of oxides, normally melt at a slightly lower temperature and these are put on first. Thus, in the firing, the darker glaze bubbles through the white or opaque glaze, and often mottled surfaces result.

If blistering or 'lifting' occurs when the second glaze is applied, allow this to dry slightly, and then press these gently down on to the pot. The glazes need to be slightly thinner than normal for double glazing.

Sgraffito

Just as it is possible to scratch through the surface of a slip to reveal a body of another colour, so it is possible to scratch through a glaze, leaving the unglazed body, or double-tip the pot in another glaze; the result is not as crisp or sharp as it is when done with slip, but it does have a softer quality not at all unpleasant.

A white tin glaze over a red body can be scratched to give pleasant results. A fairly sharp pointed tool can be used, such as a compass or pottery needle, though a pointed stick will do. It is best done when the glaze has dried completely. Often, when the glaze is scratched off, sufficient is left behind in the surface of the pot to darken it slightly and take away the raw look.

Tests

Tests should be carried out regularly, and a careful record kept. Ideally, all variations should be taken into account in each test, and only one variation allowed at a time, e.g. a new glaze needs to be tested over red

Jug with a simple scratched pattern. Lead glazed. English, mediaeval

and white bodies at different thicknesses at different temperatures. It needs to be done on flat and incised areas and on horizontal and curved surfaces. All these could be done in, say, one firing at one temperature, and a complete picture could then be built up of the different glaze effects on all these surfaces. In this example, the test glaze remains constant, while the conditions change.

Suggested glaze experiments

With a large group of students it is unusual to have sufficient weighing scales to measure out glaze tests. A good, though rough and ready way round this, is to use a volume measure. For example, plastic measuring spoons issued by baby-food manufacturers for measuring dried milk are ideal, though any small convenient measures will do. The following method has worked quite well:

1. Make test tiles in white and red clay, about 3″ × 2″, and biscuit-fire.
2. Test all materials singly to find out if any melt at 1080°C.—normal glaze-firing temperature. Suggested materials could be the lead silicates, china clay, red clay, feldspar, whiting, borax frit. It will be found that the frits melt.
3. Combine a frit with one of the other materials. A reference to the composition of a frit will show, in the case of lead monosilicate, 80 per cent lead and 20 per cent flint. As an average glaze needs alumina as well, a substance containing this will help the glaze. Thus clay is ideal but other materials can be experimented with. A typical line blend would be:

	a	b	c	d	e	f	g	h	i
Lead frit	—	1	2	3	4	5	6	7	All
Clay	All	7	6	5	4	3	2	1	—

4. When a working glaze has been found, oxides can be added to this in two ways:
a. Painting on the surface   b. Mixing with glaze
   If some students have used a borax frit and some a lead frit, the same oxides can be added to show the difference a base will make. The two different types of frits will both have their effect on the glazes.
5. When a satisfactory working glaze has been discovered, the recipe can be worked out. The measures used can be weighed and the recipe calculated in terms of percentage.

Re-glazing

Re-glazing is possible and necessary when a pot has been fired and the result is unsatisfactory, i.e. too thin, patchy, uneven. It can be re-dipped and re-fired.

Method

1. Heat the pot slowly but not too hot to make handling it uncomfortable.
2. Remove water from the top of the glaze so that it is much thicker than usual. Gum arabic or Gloy can be added to it to make it stick to the shiny surface of the pot.
3. Glaze pot in the usual way.

4. The pot when dry has a surface more fragile than usual and the slightest knock may cause the glaze to scale off. For this reason, re-glazing is only usually carried out when absolutely necessary.

Glaze faults

These are often difficult to correct in school where all the available time is required for the usual run of things and there is little time left for the consideration of technical imperfections and very time-consuming experiments which have to be carried out accurately; often the difference between success or failure is very slight.

Basically, a glaze is like a skin of the human body; it must fit without being too big or too small. When it is too small it contracts and the fault known as 'crazing' results. A maze of small hair-like cracks develops over the entire surface of the glaze. Of course, to many Chinese and Japanese potters, crazing was a feature they aimed at in their work and was often emphasised by stains being rubbed into the cracks; however, it can be insanitary and unpleasant on tableware, while being acceptable on decorative pots. The reverse of crazing, known as flaking or scaling, occurs when the skin of glaze is too big, is compressed and comes off in small pieces on rims, edges or other embellishments. Another fault is crawling, when glaze forms lumps rather than an even surface.

It is possible to change the body if all glazes are developing faults, but this is more ambitious, especially if a prepared body is being used, and is really outside the scope of most schools. So the contents of the glaze have to be considered and possible alterations made.

Crazing. Basic cure is to reduce the amount of contraction of the glaze, when cooling.

1. 2 per cent to 5 per cent flint or quartz (silica) added to the glaze will make it harder.
2. In a coloured or transparent glaze it has been found useful to add up to 2 per cent manganese.
3. Change the fluxes slightly if possible, though this is difficult in earthenware glazes. If the firing temperature is 1100°C. Zinc Oxide in small percentages can be used.
4. Try lowering the firing temperature.
5. Substitute the clay used in the recipe for clay of the body if they are not the same.

When the clay and glaze are supplied by the same firm, then they are made to fit each other, and the recommended firing temperature should be followed. If faults still occur in the glaze, and the ware has been biscuited to the correct temperature (980°C.), and remedy No. 1 has been tried without success, then contact should be made with the firm.

Peeling or flaking. This rarely happens at earthenware temperature, but I have seen it happen with a black metallic glaze saturated with copper oxide. In this particular instance the remedy would be to lower the amount of oxide. The fault generally occurs when sufficient contraction has not taken place, so to increase this the reverse methods for curing crazing are employed:

1. The silica content of the glaze is lowered.
2. The fluxes are increased.

Crawling. The glaze forms blobs rather than an even skin.
1. Ensure that biscuit ware is free from dust and grease before glazing.
2. The more viscous glazes tend to crawl rather than the freer ones; the flux may be increased slightly.
3. Try to avoid putting the glaze on too thickly, especially the highly viscous ones, e.g., white tin glaze, as they tend to be slightly more infusible.

Dryness. The glaze feels rough and unpleasant.
1. Glaze has been applied too thinly or not fired to a sufficiently high temperature.
2. Flux must be increased by the addition of lead in one of its forms, or, in a leadless glaze, by the addition of a leadless frit (i.e. Podmore's E frit).

Mattness. A form of underfired glaze which may be desired or not. It is essentially a crystalline structure, but if the glaze is to be considered as a complete and functional covering rather than a texture or pigment, it must be well fused without being at all dry. It can be induced in a glaze by an excess of alumina (clay). An addition of up to 10 per cent of clay can be tried. Any mattness which occurs accidentally may be the result of underfiring and therefore will need a higher temperature.

A matt glaze can be made glossy or slightly glossy by the increase of the flux and possibly silica and the decrease of clay (alumina).

Pinholing and blistering. Usually faults which occur during the firing. As the glaze melts, gases escape, and the different ingredients melt together to form a whole; if this is done quickly, especially at the maturing temperature, all the holes caused by escaping gases may not have had time to heat enough before cooling and vitrification begins. Blistering is usually caused by overfiring—the glaze actually boils. Little can be done except to prevent overfiring.

All glaze tests and small quantities of glaze can be added together, and the result tested on a small pot. Occasionally this gives a pleasant colour, generally dark or even black; if it is too fluid, more clay can be added, and if the colour is dull and lifeless, it can be made black with the addition of more oxides. Of course, it must be pointed out that the result is completely unrepeatable, and any additions are pure, though informed, guesswork.

The main danger with using prepared glaze stains, often temptingly listed in the manufacturer's catalogue under exotic-sounding names is that, because they have been compounded by ceramic chemists, part of the process is lost for the potter. Nowadays he has no control over the colours except to pick them out of the catalogue, rather like choosing a colour for the living-room walls. The results when used in the studio are often pale imitations of industrial glazes; while these glazes appear to offer a wide range of colours, many of them are crude and dull. Try, as much as possible, to mix and experiment with the raw materials, rather than use the factory goods. The results will give more satisfaction than all the fancy glaze stains supplied. Our aim, surely, is not to compete with the garish colours of many mass-produced wares, but to help individuals to seek out and explore possibilities for themselves.

8 Firing

Clay has to be subjected to heat either in an open fire or a kiln to render it insoluble in water; this is known as firing. If the temperature is sufficiently high, it will also render the clay completely impervious. During a firing, both physically and chemically combined water is driven off and a chemical change takes place in the clay.

The chemical formula for pure clay is $Al_2O_3 \cdot 2SiO_2 \cdot 2H_2O$ i.e. it is composed of one part of alumina, two of silica and two of water. If it is subjected to a sufficiently high temperature it will actually melt and sag. The melting point of clay depends upon the flux or impurities present and in refractory clays it is very high indeed. Most earthenware clays will not stand a temperature of much more than 1100°C. without warping. Red clays, because of their iron content, about 8 per cent, have a particularly restricted firing range and at about 1100°C. they begin to vitrify—a general fusion of the molecules takes place which renders the body practically waterproof; if the temperature continues to increase the clay bloats and eventually melts and collapses. Few earthenware bodies become completely impervious and a glaze is needed to complete the process of waterproofing.

Firing temperature of clays

The various names given to types of bodies can be roughly divided into three groups:

1 Earthenware consists of pots fired up to 1150°C. Few clays are completely vitrified at this temperature, though the red ones do vitrify. The glaze remains as a skin on the surface.

2 Stoneware is usually fired up to 1300°C., though 1280°C. is the average. The clay is invariably vitrified and the glaze combines with the clay to give a much tougher non-porous body. The colours available are more limited, as most colouring oxides burn away before this temperature is reached.

1 Earthenware pot with applied decoration. English 1707

2 Left: Stoneware dish with brushwork decoration. English 1950

3 Porcelain bowl

4 Tea bowl with brown black glaze. Japanese Raku

5 Salt-glaze jug, showing the arms of Queen Elizabeth 1. German, 1594

3 Porcelain is the name given to the pure white translucent ware fired above this temperature. The body vitrifies completely to give it the characteristic translucency. The resulting body is very hard and is capable of being made into very fine thin ware. Industrially, it is used in the production of such things as electrical insulators, laboratory equipment, etc. Pure white china clay, free from impurities forms the body, and to it a flux, such as feldspar, is added.

4 Raku is a low temperature ware fired very quickly by being put into a glowing furnace until it is red hot. To withstand the tremendous shock of this type of firing, the body must be extremely open to allow the molecules to expand rapidly and allow moisture to escape quickly. It was widely used by the Japanese for producing tea bowls.

5 Salt-glaze ware is unique in that it has only one firing and a glaze is formed without any of the usual ingredients. It is used nowadays in the manufacture of sewage pipes, etc. though during the seventeenth century it was used widely in England for the production of domestic pottery; it was used before that during the middle ages in Germany. Stoneware clay is used and, near the end of the firing, ordinary salt is introduced into the kiln, which vaporises, settles on the pots and combines with the clay on the surface to form a hard acid-resistant glaze. Unfortunately the fumes are highly poisonous and the process cannot be done in an electric kiln as the fumes attack the elements, nor can any other kiln be used for an ordinary firing once salt has been introduced, as it settles on the walls of the kiln and continues to vaporise during each firing. The ware is fired, once only, to about 1250°–1280°C.

6 Heat-resisting ware which can be put directly on to a flame fall into two types.

a. *Low-fired earthenware* The clay is soft terra cotta and when fired is extremely open. The outside is normally unglazed and the ware is fired to around 1000°C. Such pots are made in Southern France and in Northern and Eastern Spain. The open body allows the rapid expansion of the molecules to take place without causing the body to crack. The clay may also contain a high proportion of talc or steatite which is unaffected by heat.

b. *High-fired ware* Usually made from fine porcelain. The body is usually very thin and this conducts the heat through it rapidly, enabling it to withstand the shock of rapid expansion, e.g. laboratory evaporating dishes.

6 Red earthenware cooking pot. Moroccan

The first or biscuit firing

This renders the pot insoluble in water.

Pots need to be fired twice because:

1. It is much easier to glaze and decorate biscuit rather than 'raw' ware, as biscuit ware is much stronger.
2. Many clays cannot be 'raw' glazed without collapsing, as glazes generally need to be applied fairly thickly.

A biscuit-fired pot has had all the chemically combined water driven off, and this has left small gaps between the molecules. These gaps make the walls very porous and water is quickly, almost instantly, drawn into them, both by the action of capillarity and absorption. This is why, when the pot is dipped into the liquid glaze, it sticks to the surface, and why soluble salts in a glaze cannot be used.

The biscuit firing is the slowest of the firings, and in studio pottery it is to the lowest temperature, the usual one being about 980°C. The reverse is true in the pottery industry. Here space and firing expenses are important, and kilns can be packed much tighter and fuller for a biscuit firing, because the pots can be packed inside each other without fear of them sticking. While this method would probably be more economical for individual potters, it does have problems: as the clay is fired to the higher temperature, it becomes non-porous and does not absorb the glaze. In industry, this problem can be overcome by completely mechanized processes and so firing costs are reduced.

For our purposes, then, we use the lower temperature for biscuit ware and the higher one for glazing. The kiln is packed when the pots are thoroughly dry. Each pot needs to be checked for any faults, such as split handles and warping. If a crack or split has developed round the handle, which means that the pot was probably too hard when the handle was put on, it should be smoothed over with a damp sponge and pressed down with a tool. Rough edges should also be smoothed over and any shavings or cuttings of clay adhering to the pot should be removed. Some potters use fine wire wool for this purpose, but you must be careful that no iron bits get into the clay reclaim.

The pots can be packed inside each other, or, in the case of mugs, rim to rim. The aim is to be as economical as possible with space, while allowing room for the moisture to escape and the pots to expand and contract while firing. Pots with very thick bases should not be packed inside each other.

Avoid placing heavy pots on thinner ones, especially on the rims, or splitting may occur. Pots placed inside each other must not be fitted tightly, or all the gases, especially those produced by carbon, will not be able to escape and this may cause trouble in the glaze firing. As pots shrink after firing, one pot could get stuck inside another.

The kiln is made up with shelves or batts supported on props. Use as few of these as possible, building up pots on top of each other. Finally the cone (temperature indicator) needs to be placed in front of the spy hole. If the kiln is fitted with a pyrometer, which is a dial showing the heat inside the kiln, no cones are necessary. Cones should be supported by a ring of clay round their base.

The first firing should be slow to allow all the changes to take place thoroughly without damage being done to the ware. Thick coil pots or models need a slower firing than the thinner walled pots.

Firing schedule

100°C	Water driven off as vapour. Any wax burns away.
350°–500°C.	Chemically combined water is driven off. Any organic material burns away.
500°–600°C.	Change in chemical structure of clay which is irreversible, but body still very fragile and crumbly.
980°C.	Body change sufficient to make clay hard yet still porous. Usual temperature of biscuit firing. (Cone OA7.)
1080°–1100°C.	Average earthenware temperature. Most earthenware glazes have matured.
1150°C.	Limit of red clay body and most clays begin to vitrify.

The start of a firing must be very slow. Any moisture in the clay, or in air bubbles, must be given plenty of chance to escape before boiling point is reached, or it will cause splitting or even exploding. From then on the firing can be speeded up until 500°C. when the silica begins to change. From 600°C. a dark red glow begins in the kiln and when this is spread evenly throughout, the firing can be speeded up until the cone melts and falls over indicating that the temperature has been reached.

Ideally, a graph showing the rise in temperature should be made, and this is possible to work out if a pyrometer is fitted. The vertical scale can show the temperature and the horizontal scale the time and temperature control indicator. This gives the whole firing interest, acts as a guide if the pyrometer or cones fail, and shows if economical use is being made of the kiln. A firing-log, too, is useful. A record showing the date and time the kiln is switched on, the control settings and the time the temperature was reached are sufficient. If the kiln has its own meter, a reading of this can be taken, and the amount of units used calculated. This log, and the kiln graph, will show any discrepancies in the firings, besides recording how often the kiln is used.

Cooling should follow a similar cycle, but in reverse. Fairly fast cooling down to 600°C., slow cooling down to 450°C., rapid down to 200°C., and then slow to 100°C. Continual rapid cooling must be avoided, or 'dunting' (cracking) of the pots may take place. If the kiln is fitted with a ventilation brick and a pyrometer, the cooling can vary as shown, but if no pyrometer is fitted it is best to allow cooling to take place slowly. It usually takes a kiln as long to cool as it does to heat up, though the times do vary slightly.

All these recommendations are based on electric kilns, though all firing cycles are similar. New kilns usually have a recommended firing schedule supplied by the manufacturers, and this should be followed, especially for the first few firings. They will also, probably, help with suggestions as to how the kiln can be fired in relationship to special circumstances, such as school closing at four o'clock.

When considering how long a kiln is going to take to fire, the pack or content must be reckoned with. If this is open, with tall pots, the firing may go much quicker than when the kiln is packed with shelves and small pots.

A new kiln is usually supplied with the furniture it requires, that is shelves and props. If new or replacement furniture has to be ordered, choose the high temperature variety. Earthenware shelves and props will not withstand stoneware temperatures and should there be a disaster and the kiln get overfired, everything in the kiln, including shelves and props, will be ruined. If, however, the shelves made out of sillimanite for high temperatures are in use, they will survive; the initial cost is little more, yet they have all the advantages of withstanding high temperatures.

When packing the kiln, shelves should be packed so that about $\frac{1}{2}$" of space is left above the pots to allow for any initial expansion of the ware. It is a good idea to coat the top of the shelves with a batt-wash of some kind. This can either be a proprietary mix, or, much cheaper and just as effective, is a mixture of half china clay and flint. Painted on to the shelf, fairly thickly, it helps to prevent glaze sticking to the shelf, as it acts as a barrier. A wire brush is useful for removing bits of clay or glaze from the surface of the shelf, and on no account must fingers be rubbed over shelf surface, as tiny splinters of glaze have edges sharper than razors.

Shelves need only three props for support, not four. This means that fewer props are required, leaving more room in the kiln for pots, and the shelf will not wobble on three supports, while it may on four.

Fire-clay, a highly refractory clay found near coal seams, can be used to pad worn props or shelves. Small balls of fire-clay, pressed flat and dipped in sand, make useful levellers.

Shelf props

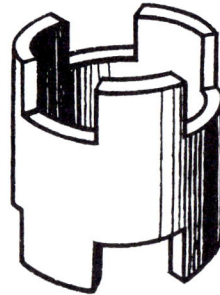

Glaze firing

Much more care is needed when a glaze (or glost) kiln is being packed. Pots must not touch each other and each one must be checked to ensure the glaze has not been chipped or damaged and that no glaze remains on the foot if spurs are not used. Besides which, each pot, especially if it has decoration, must be handled carefully to prevent smudging. Sort out beforehand those pots which are the same height so that they can go on to the same shelves. This will save time when the actual packing begins. Underpack rather than overpack to prevent pots from sticking together.

A cone (see below) is more important in a glaze firing, as the temperature must be accurate. It is placed in front of the spy-hole in the kiln, and

it is useful, especially if children are watching the kiln, to put in two cones, one melting at a lower temperature than that required; this first one acts as a warning to watch the kiln carefully. Even if a pyrometer is fitted, it is as well to use a cone for a glaze firing.

The firing can go much faster this time as there is no chemically combined water, but the silica change around 500°–600°C. happens as before so this period needs a steady rise. After this the controls can be turned up rapidly.

Check the kiln hourly until it is glowing brightly, then half-hourly, and when it looks as if it is ready for maturing, every fifteen minutes. A cone has matured when it is 'touching its toes'.

Cones are triangular pyramids of compressed glaze material, which are calculated to melt and fall over at a given temperature. They were originally invented by a German called Seger in the last century, and are often known as Seger cones. They are reliable but must be stored in a dry place as damp can affect their reaction. A cone, once used, whether it reached the temperature or not, should not be re-used.

Cones have a number on them indicating the temperature at which they fall. Seger invented the cones from 1100°C. upwards, and these are usually known by a number only, but sometimes have a prefix H, which could mean 'hard', i.e. 1100°C.–Cone 1 or H1, the temperature rises are either 20° or 30°. For temperatures below 1100°C. the numbers work in the opposite direction–1060°C. is cone 02 and 980°C. is Cone 06. These numbers always have the letter 'O' before them.

Table showing cones, temperature, colour in kiln and the associated bodies and glazes

Cone	Temperature (Centigrade)	Colour in kiln	Body and glaze
022	600°	Just begins to show dull red	Most enamels and lustres
018	710°		
016	750°		
015	790°	Red	Soft glazes, the harder enamels, i.e. pink
010	900°		
08	940°	Dull cherry	Biscuit temperatures for studio ware
07	960°		
06	980°		
04	1020°	Light cherry	Most earthenware glazes
03	1040°		
02	1060°		
01	1080°		
1	1100°	Dark to pale orange	Industrial earthenware biscuit
5	1180°		
6	1200°	Lemon	Medium stoneware
8	1250°	Yellowish white	Stoneware
9	1280°		
11	1320°	White	Porcelain

Firing enamels and lustres

When enamels are being fired, which need a much lower temperature than usual, about 750°C., the kiln must have good ventilation or be fired with the door slightly open (which is dangerous in a classroom, and should be watched closely) to allow fumes to escape; otherwise these can settle on elements and cause them to burn out.

Kiln controls

Controls on an electric kiln vary, depending mainly upon its size. Many are fitted with a control rather like that on an electric hot-plate: off, low, medium and full—and in a small kiln this can be quite sufficient and is a cheap method of control. The biggest disadvantage is that the control puts on at a time only a few of the heating elements of the kiln, rather than all the elements on a quarter or half strength. For this, a more expensive piece of equipment is necessary. However, the cheaper kind is usually adequate, and on a large kiln the low can be left on all night or the kiln switched on early in the morning, left on low for a couple of hours, medium for a couple of hours, then turned up to full.

The more expensive type of temperature control is known as a heat input regulator. This controls all the elements and switches them on and off for a set length of time. Usually the control has a dial marked from 0 to 100. At 0 it is off, and at 1 it is on for 1 unit out of 100 units, at 33 it is on for a third and off for two-thirds, etc. At 100 it is on continually. The units may be seconds or more, but usually the units are not defined. Assuming that 1 unit=one second, it works by switching itself on, if set on 1, for one second and off for 99. The changes on the dial must be manually operated, i.e., the control changed from 30 to 60, say, though it is possible to order programme controllers which will complete the firing cycle by slowing periods down and speeding others up and eventually, switching off at the required temperature. These are naturally very expensive. Energy or input regulators are expensive and are only necessary for a large kiln which may need to be left on overnight. Pyrometers are of great value. The rise in temperature can be seen and checked frequently and if a cone is used, it acts as a double check, especially if the pyrometer is at the back of the kiln. The table on page 85 shows the colours which may be found in a normal firing and, as experience grows, they can be recognised more easily.

Kilns

A kiln is merely a vehicle by which heat is applied to a pot. Its main advantage over an open fire is that it protects pots from the flame, while allowing control to be exercised over the temperature.

Of course, electric kilns have every advantage from an earthenware potter's point of view, yet for more ambitious schools who want to venture into the field of stoneware and controlled atmospheres, they can be very dull. Traditionally, kilns have been fired with wood, whereas nowadays, gas, coke and oil are used. All these kilns need much more expensive installation with a flue and a chimney of some kind. Each has advantages, though for earthenware, these do not apply.

Basically, firing cycles are the same, and the heat is controlled by the amount of fuel used. The main difference in construction between electric and other kilns is that whereas an electric kiln is simply a box with heating elements round the inside walls, a gas, wood or coke kiln must have protection for the pots from the flames, which would affect the glazes. This is done by means of a muffle round which the flames go.

However, for occasional firings and for the joy of completing the whole process, it is quite simple to build a kiln and operate a firing.

The simplest and most direct method of firing unglazed ware, which

Simple, brick built, updraught kiln

must go back many thousands of years, is in an open fire. The pots are laid on wood and the fire is made over them; this needs to be kept slow at first and at the end needs to be covered over with leaves, grass or hay to prevent draughts from getting at the pots. Only clay containing a good opener, such as grog or sand, can withstand the shock of this type of firing, and the pots will reach only a low temperature, say 750°C., but this is quite sufficient to render them usable although still very porous.

The next, but slightly more complicated method, is the updraught kiln. A trench is dug in the ground for the fire and over this a chamber is built. Fire bricks are necessary as ordinary bricks will not take the strain without splintering. A round chamber can be built up and the top closed in to a small hole to allow the smoke and heat to escape. The fire, built underneath the chamber, needs to be slow at first, and eventually quite a good temperature may be reached. Naturally, glazed ware cannot be fired this way, nor will the pots look clean when they are out; the flames will have left them black, brown, red, mottled, etc. Nor can the temperature be checked in any way, unless a spyhole is left and a cone put inside. The draught can be controlled to some extent by opening or closing the opening at the top of the chamber.

Many variations on this method can be made; iron bands can be used for banding the bricks together, etc., but it is unlikely that the kiln will withstand many firings.

Another method, involving the use of a saggar (a box with no top, made out of refractory clay, used to hold pots in wood fired kilns without muffles, to protect them from the flames), is built up on the bricks, surrounded on three sides by bricks coming in to form a narrow chimney. Pots are put inside the saggar, the front blocked up with a kiln shelf or with bricks. Coke enables a good temperature to be reached quite quickly.

Updraught kiln

pots inside a large plant pot

coke fire made underneath

Saggar kiln

coke fire

Top plan of saggar

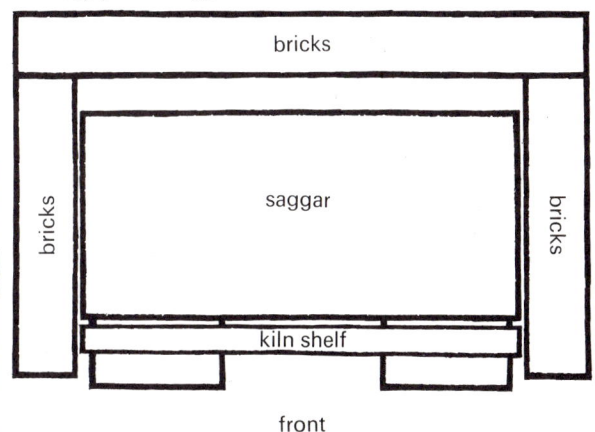

bricks

bricks

saggar

bricks

kiln shelf

front

9 Equipment and materials

This chapter is an attempt to serve as a guide to what is essential from the outset, and what can be left until later. It is surprising what a small amount of equipment is really vital to a pottery, yet, to do the job well, some is desirable without being necessary. With a limited amount of money available, it is up to the individual teacher to decide what has to be bought and what can be improvised. (For the names and addresses of suppliers see Appendix 2, page 110.)

Most of the notes apply to the secondary school, either starting a pottery or planning a new one. The infant school may already have tables which are suitable, and clay is the only material necessary unless a kiln is available. In the primary school, the basic equipment would be useful, though again clay is the only vital material, unless a kiln is available, in which case glaze materials and kiln furniture will be necessary.

Tables

Tables need to be strong and firm, and the top easily washable—formica or similar strong plastic surfaces are ideal. A wooden surface has great advantages for clay work in that it is slightly absorbent and this prevents the clay from sticking when one is wedging and kneading. An ideal combination would be one table with a wooden surface and the remainder with smooth and easy to clean surfaces. Zinc-topped tables, usually supplied for science laboratories in school, are very good; the zinc gives the table weight which is good for clay preparation, and is also smooth.

Stools

Stools are required when fine modelling is being done. Chairs are usually too low, and the backs tend to take up too much space and prevent movement. Usually neither chairs nor stools are necessary, as most work can only be done standing up.

Sinks

Water is essential in a pottery, and if a supply of hot water is available, washing up is made much easier. The continuous type of gas geyser is excellent, if hot water from a central system is not available, as other types of water heater tend to run cold very quickly.

Two sinks are desirable, placed at opposite ends of the pottery, so that access to a sink can be quick and more children can get at one. The flat rather than the deep sink is useful.

Towels

Towels are necessary, but do get filthy very quickly. Roller towels changed daily, paper towels, or automatic roller towels, are ideal.

Fitted furniture

As a rule, this needs to be kept to a minimum in any practical room, so that changes can be made to fit various situations. However, in the planning of a new pottery, fitted benches round the walls are very useful. The cupboard space can store all the equipment and the tops provide good working surfaces. Points for gas and electricity can be fitted and used as necessary.

Plaster slabs

Plaster slabs cannot usually be ordered, but have to be made on the spot. Usually they are required to dry out clay which has been reclaimed and for kneading wet clay. There are two solutions to this problem:

a. To have a table with a plaster surface. An old woodwork bench is ideal, with a 3" layer of plaster on the top. The disadvantage is that the plaster cannot be replaced quickly when damaged.

b. A series of plaster slabs, 3" thick and about 3' × 2' can provide a satisfactory alternative; they can quickly be replaced when damaged and dried out thoroughly from time to time by being placed near a radiator. They can be made either in a suitable cardboard box or in a frame resting on glass—this gives a beautifully smooth surface. Try to keep separate slabs for separate clays, e.g. white and red.

Old or new woodwork benches are excellent for wedging and preparing clay, and should the opportunity of acquiring one arise, it should be accepted.

Clay bins and clay storage

Clay delivered from a supplier will usually be delivered in its plastic form, wrapped in polythene, and virtually ready to use. It will usually remain in good condition when well wrapped until it is required for use. It is best stored in a cool, damp place, but if it has to be kept in the pottery room, keep it away from the kiln and any radiators.

As the clay is used, a bin will be required to keep the odd bits and returned work. A baby's old bath, covered with a damp cloth and a sheet of polythene is an efficient improvisation, but ideally bins with well fitting lids are required. Some education authorities (e.g. the ILEA) supply square bins about 3' high which are very good, otherwise galvanized zinc dustbins are suitable; all need a wooden grid in the bottom to allow a layer of water, which will keep the contents damp, to remain separate from the clay. If the clay in the bin is covered with a damp cloth, any hard clay will be softened, and over a holiday, for instance, the clay will be kept in good condition. Any clay which has hardened into a leather-hard state (but not dried out completely) can be cut and broken into slices and lumps, sprinkled with water, covered with a damp cloth, and will be in a good working state after a few days if the cloth is kept damp.

A bin is required for each type of clay used, e.g. white, red, and grogged clay would need three bins, as the grogged clay should be kept quite separate. Two small bins or buckets, with lids (to prevent foreign bodies from entering) can be used for storing any clay which has dried altogether, e.g. reclaimed clay. These buckets can also hold the slurry from the wheel, which needs to be allowed to settle before the surplus water is poured or siphoned off. Clay softened down in this way can be spread out on plaster slabs to dry. When clay is in this state, it is a particularly good time to add grog or sand if work on coil or slab pots is planned; this ensures that the clay and grog are thoroughly mixed. Obviously, as the clay is wet, its dry weight is unknown, so it will always be a matter of guesswork as to how much grog needs to be added, but, assuming a water content of 50 per cent, an addition of 10 per cent dry grog to the clay (as estimated dry) is usually sufficient; add it to the bucket and stir well. Grogged clay must be kept separate from the ordinary clay, so some care needs to be exercised, and separate bins and buckets made available. Some dried clay from unfinished pots should be kept and can be used in recipes for glaze and slip when clay is needed.

Damp cupboard

A damp cupboard of some sort is essential to keep work from one week to the next, as it is not always possible to complete work in one session. A damp cupboard, meaning a container to hold work which has to remain damp, can be fabricated from any ordinary cupboard by lining it with polythene sheets. If possible, the base should contain a tray of water to help keep the atmosphere damp, though bricks soaked and filled with water will do. Ideally, a damp room should be included in all new pottery rooms, or an old storeroom might be converted. The walls need to be lined with shelves at various heights to allow for tiles, tall pots, etc. As in the damp cupboard, some kind of humidifier is required. The door needs to be as airtight as possible and kept closed. Additional sheets of polythene are needed to wrap up work such as coil pots, but this presents difficulties with pots which are very soft, e.g. thrown pots.

There are two solutions:

a. Allow the pots to harden slightly before wrapping them up, which means a return visit later in the day.

b. Cover them with a biscuit tin.

If no damp cupboard or room is available, biscuit tins can be used and are reasonably efficient, though they do tend to take up a lot of space.

Work put into the damp cupboard or room needs to be clearly labelled with the owner's name, both on the pot and on the outside covering. This is especially applicable when wrapped in polythene as it cannot be recognized without being unwrapped and possibly damaged. Also, as work dries out, it shrinks down and is often difficult to recognize, especially if a group of children have produced similar work.

Buckets

Buckets are required for the storage of slips, glazes and possibly clay. These, for preference, should be polythene with well-fitting lids to prevent evaporation and to keep out foreign bodies. Lids can be improvised from pieces of hardboard cut to size. Polythene is more practical than enamel, as it is quiet, smooth, and unbreakable. Large sweet jars can also be used for storing glaze and slip.

Bowls

Bowls are essential. Large ones for glazing larger pots could be enamel, while medium and small, basin-type should be in plastic. One small basin-type bowl per person is ideal and is a convenient size for water and slip in small quantities.

Banding wheels

These are expensive, about £3 each, but are very useful, as work can be turned round constantly while being built and decorated. They are especially useful when coil pots are being built, and for model work. A wheel for each child is ideal.

Phosphor bronze sieves

At least one is essential for the preparation of slips and glazes. Ready mixed glazes need only be put through a 60 mesh sieve, though some potters use a 120. Slips need a 60 or 80 mesh. An 8"/80 mesh sieve is the bare minimum, and will serve all purposes.

The number indicates the number of holes per square inch, and as the sieves are expensive, care must be exercised in their use. Avoid over-

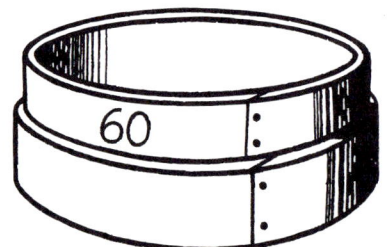

Glaze brush – fairly long bristles

Japanese paintbrush – soft full hair

Glaze mop – soft full hair

Sieving brush – long stiff bristles

filling and pressing the mesh, which may stretch. Use a brush to help the glaze or slip through. A nail or scrub brush is good, kept specially for the purpose.

Glaze brushes

These can be purchased – usually quite cheaply, without being specially necessary.

Glaze mops

These are large, full bodied brushes for applying glaze. Beautifully soft and useful. Expensive.

Underglaze brushes

These have hair in a quill to prevent metal corrosion. They often have odd names: liners are flat, shaders are pointed, tracers are long and pointed, etc. All are available in various sizes.

Japanese brushes are beautiful for brush work on pots, and need careful use; they are very expensive but beautifully balanced, and a pleasure to use.

Tiles or asbestos squares

These are required for work in progress. Ordinary kitchen tiles 6"×6", glazed on one side, are particularly useful. The glazed side is good for sliding on thrown pots, while the unglazed side is good for building pots and models, as the clay does not stick: if the tile is soaked in water beforehand, this will help to keep the pot damp. Asbestos has the advantage of being less fragile, and can be used in almost any size, besides being cheaper.

Rolling pins

These need to be sufficiently long to roll out large pieces of clay. Plain wooden ones, without any special handles are best. Ordinary poles of wood, if smooth, will do, provided they are sufficiently thick. Metal scaffolding, if the clay is not too wet, will also work well.

Deck chair canvas

This is ideal for rolling out clay on, and it can be used to lift it into position if necessary. Hessian, or clean sacking, is good, but gives a larger texture pattern. For rolling out clay only, paper (sugar or cartridge) is ideal.

Rolling guides

These are needed to support the rolling pin and enable an even thickness of clay to be rolled out, can either be purchased from a supplier or from a timber merchant, 18" long and 1" wide×$\frac{1}{4}$" or $\frac{5}{8}$" thick, depending on the size required. These guides are useful for supporting sieves or pots over buckets.

Slicing guides

These are for slicing blocks of clay evenly, and are usually made of wood: they need to be $\frac{1}{2}$"×$\frac{3}{4}$"×6" and have even saw marks down the edge to hold the cutting wire.

Wires

These are essential for cutting clay and trimming pots. Brass wire is strong and can be bought in a coil and made into wires, using toggles or 2" lengths of $\frac{1}{4}$" dowelling rod with a hole drilled through the centre.

Single strands are required for slicing or trimming, while double or twisted wire is much stronger for wedging and general use. A double wire is made by fastening two or more lengths of wire to two toggles, putting one end on to a weight and spinning it round. The wire will twist evenly together. All wires need to have the ends turned back from the centre, so that when they are pulled across the clay, the sharp ends do not go into the fingers.

Nylon fishing line is an excellent substitute for a single wire as it is very strong, but it is usually too thick for trimming the tops of pots.

Pestles and mortars
For grinding up oxides and underglaze colours these are useful. They are expensive and sold by the size.

Sponges
Sponges of various sorts are essential. Small, fine, natural sponges for smoothing edges and mopping water out of thrown pots, are expensive, and should be used only for that purpose. Large, synthetic sponges are excellent for cleaning tables, while smaller ones can be used for wiping glaze etc. from biscuit ware.

Modelling tools
Tools made from boxwood are essential, and should be kept clean. Sets of a dozen can be bought. Wire-ended tools are expensive, but are good for hollowing out models.

Scales
For weighing out raw materials, can be either the spring balance type or the ordinary balance type, using either ounces or grammes. A chemical balance, using grammes, is necessary for weighing very small amounts of oxides, and for carrying out glaze tests, which must be accurate.

Knives
Plenty of knives for cutting up slabs, etc. are invaluable. Any sort of kitchen knife will do. Clay wears away metal very quickly, so the cheaper the better.

Rulers
For measuring slabs etc. rulers are useful, and can be either cheap wooden ones, or expensive metal ones, which wear very well.

Tools
Pliers for cutting wire; hammer.

Paint scrapers
These are needed for lifting pots from the wheel and cleaning benches.

Slip trailers
Different types can be purchased, beside home-made ones. The bulb type, as explained in Chapter 1, is perhaps the best. Plastic bottles fitted with nozzles are very good, and cheap. Babies' feeding bottles, fitted with a cork and a nozzle, are simple to make and operate. Avoid allowing slip to dry in the nozzles, as this is difficult to wash out; wash them immediately after use. Enema syringes, bought at the chemists, are also very good.

Wheels
1 Kick wheels. Many varieties of this type are available. (Prices usually start around £30.) Basically there are two types—standing and sitting.

a. *Standing type.* The potter stands on one leg and kicks with the other. Disadvantages:

1. With only one foot on the ground it is difficult to keep good balance.

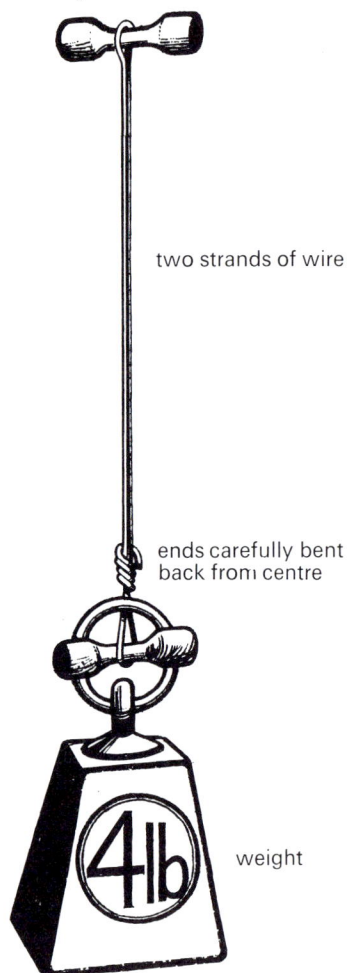

Making a twisted wire

two strands of wire

ends carefully bent back from centre

weight

Pestle and mortar

2. Large pots are difficult to manage.

3. The fly-wheel is often inadequate, and a good speed cannot be maintained.

Advantages:

1. Quite cheap.

2. Takes up less space.

Best of this type: Wenger.

b. *Sit-down type.* These wheels are roughly triangular in shape with the seat at the pointed end, across which the potter sits, using one leg for kicking. They are the more traditional type of wheel.

Disadvantages:

1. Costs much more money.

2. Takes up more space.

Advantages:

1. The body is well balanced and full, relaxed control can be exercised.

2. The work is less tiring.

3. This kind of wheel tends to be larger and fitted with much more efficient fly-wheel.

4. There is a much happier relationship between machine and body.

2 Electric wheels. Again there are many firms producing different varieties (most prices beginning around £70). Most are fitted with a seat, which is removable. Mechanically, there are two types:

a. *Cone-driven*   b. *Wheel-driven*

The cone-driven wheel is capable of dealing with heavier loads as the machine rate remains constant, with the speed being varied by cones rather like gears; the wheel-driven type has its speed controlled by the machine, which reduces speed.

Most important, the wheel should be capable of a minimum speed of 30–40 revolutions per minute, to allow large pots to be made, without any loss in driving force. Most wheels are uneven at low speeds, which are the most important ones, while they are excellent at the higher speeds required for centring. They should be capable of dealing with a lump of 15–20 lb without any speed loss at all speeds.

Of course, though this should go without saying, they should be perfectly safe electrically.

The electric wheel, supplied by Judson and Hudson, Ltd, Keighley, Yorkshire, which is cone-driven, is very satisfactory.

Which wheel—kick or electric?

Ideally, both are necessary; a kick wheel is more direct, and responds instantly to speed changes, while an electric wheel takes a few seconds and is much more a machine intervening between worker and material. A kick wheel, however, does require control of two techniques—throwing, and kicking, which need to be learned, while with an electric one, full concentration can be applied to the throwing technique.

If a decision had to be made between the two, an electric one is, perhaps, more useful in school. If this is too expensive, the Leach type wheel (see p. 47) is very good.

A standing kick wheel would be the least desirable choice because although it is cheap it is unsatisfactory. The most successful method of managing it is to have two students on it at one time — one throwing and the other kicking.

Many wheels in use in schools are often totally inadequate for the job. Throwing is a sophisticated and highly skilled technique demanding well designed and efficient machines, and all the considerations mentioned above need to be taken into account when a choice is made.

Kilns

Many different kinds of kiln are produced, and a wide choice is available.

This section deals with electric kilns only. Electric kilns have these advantages:

1. No flues are necessary.
2. Temperature is easily controlled and simple to operate.
3. Safe in use.
4. Easily fitted with the minimum of installation.

Should plans be made for firing to stoneware temperature, a gas kiln is to be recommended.

For any school that wishes to build its own kiln (electric or oil), The Saviac Workshop supplies plans which are fully explained and detailed, and are economically designed to combine maximum efficiency with minimum cost.

Electric kilns. Two types. a. Side loading   b. Top loading

On the whole the side loading has the advantage.

a. *Side loading*

Advantages:

1., Much easier to see how packing is going, and how closely the shelves can be packed.
2. Much faster to pack.

Disadvantages:

1. Doors containing elements have wiring which has to be movable but is usually contained in a flexible conduit pipe. Door elements are exposed while packing is in progress and therefore likely to be damaged.
2. The door may not be as well fitting as it should be, and currents of cold air may result.

b. *Top loading*

Advantages:

1. Elements go all round walls with no interference.
2. No side door, therefore can occupy smaller space.

Disadvantages:

1. Difficult to pack.
2. Lid usually heavy, especially for children.
3. A convenient adult height is too high for children.

Kiln size. When planning a pottery the size of the kiln must be related to the amount of work to be produced. For example, is it going to be more satisfactory to have a smaller kiln fired constantly, or a bigger kiln fired more infrequently? A quick turnover of work is very desirable, especially from a child's point of view, when results are important. Yet the kiln must be large enough to deal quickly with pots of a good size, of say, 18".

Again, if the pottery is small and the kiln has to be in one corner, it is no good allotting half the space to it: large kilns usually need a room of their own.

In general, the size depends on individual circumstances. If the department is ambitious and the money is available, choose a large kiln, but if a more modest programme is planned, it may be much better to order a medium size. Small kilns are, on the whole, uneconomical as far as the initial cost goes and the amount of work they can deal with. If pottery is going to be considered as a minor activity in the school then a small kiln may be the answer.

Points for consideration

a. A medium-size kiln with an internal chamber of 18"×18"×18" costs around £120.

A large kiln, with a firing space 24"×30"×30" costs around £300.

b. A kiln needs to be evident in the pottery and be an integral part of it, rather than something slightly sacred, which only the teacher deals with. Therefore it is ideally situated in the pottery itself or in a room immediately adjacent to it, rather than at the other end of the school.

c. Large kilns need an energy input control, costing around £26. Medium kilns can be operated safely on a manual low/med/high control.

d. All kilns need to be fitted by a qualified electrician and manufacturer's instructions carried out.

Kiln furniture. This consists of shelves and props. These are usually supplied with the kiln, and additional or replacement ones purchased. It is advisable to purchase furniture suitable for high temperature work, as this does wear better than low temperature furniture, and if the kiln is overfired, it will not be ruined.

Pyrometers (heat indicators with the dial fitted on the outside of the kiln) are essential if the temperature is to be constantly checked.

Should stoneware temperatures be planned, then the kiln should be equipped for this from the beginning, as special high temperature elements are used. These, of course, operate perfectly at all other temperatures.

Local sources of clay

These depend very largely upon the area and the surrounding industries. Local patches of clay found over the country can be tested for suitability. Most will fire well at earthenware temperatures, though they may need additions to make them workable, e.g. if they are short or contain too much sand, ordinary white ball clay or terra cotta will help; if too sticky or soapy, add sand. However, most of the clay which is revealed by roadworks etc., while good, is difficult to obtain in large quantities, and may involve the teacher in plenty of work, so, while it is an excellent plan to use some and encourage children to bring in clay, as a long term plan it has difficulties.

Local factories using clay are often a good cheap source for the regular bodies, e.g. brick works, pipe and saltglaze works, clay pipe manufacturers. The bodies are often quite rough, with an interesting texture rarely found in the 'machine-made' clay from the supplier.

Boy aged 13 at work on a model of a church

10 Pottery in school

Pottery now forms a part of the curriculum of many schools: in some it is taught alongside art, while in others it is offered as an alternative to it. It is important for those teachers who find themselves able to include pottery in their syllabus to know two things. First, the reasons for teaching pottery in school and second, how to carry out all the many and complicated processes involved in dealing with clay. The preceding chapters of this book have been concerned with the processes and this chapter is concerned with the reasons.

Since the first part of this century when, under the influence of such people as Professor Cizek, the value of children's painting came to be recognised, art has come to be regarded as a valuable part of the educative process. The purpose and position of craft work on the other hand have never been so clearly defined. There seem on the whole to be two different methods of teaching craft. The traditional craftsman, teaching such crafts as woodwork, metalwork and needlework, limits most of the teaching to that of technique. Preconceived designs are carried out by children under the close supervision of the teacher. Little original work is encouraged and the exercises carried out cover only a limited number of techniques. At the other end of the scale is the experimenter—he uses materials for his own ends. With little or no technical skill or knowledge, he uses wood, cloth or clay for his own purposes with no reference to their traditional use. Sometimes such experiments yield fascinating results but usually they fail through lack of skill.

Pottery is, together with wood and metalwork, one of the most ancient and historic crafts of man. Wood was cut and used for building houses, metal was hammered into tools and clay was moulded into storage pots or drinking vessels. Craftsmen of different sorts have long been an integral part of society.

Today the situation is slightly different. Mass production has eliminated the need for most of these crafts. Ready-made clothing, furniture, tools, and even pre-cooked food have, if people so desire, removed the need for all these old traditional crafts. However, the do-it-yourself shops flourish and grow, more and more magazines are published on how to cook exotic meals; clothing and furnishing materials get better and brighter designs, and pottery classes expand and increase. It would seem that there are still a lot of people who have a desire to make things for themselves.

Granted this, we must still try to answer the question, 'Why teach pottery in school?' and the related question, 'How should we teach it?'

In her book *Creative Crafts in Education*, Seonaid Robertson gives two reasons for teaching pottery in school. I quote them here because they seem to me to be of paramount importance.

(1) Crafts make their chief contribution to education as a form of the arts, that is, as a vehicle for the revelation of the human spirit and (2) that they make it in a widely acceptable and tangible form in the creation of a satisfying environment.

These two basic points need, I think, to be dealt with in more detail.
1. Craftwork is a practical branch of the arts and as such provides a framework for expression and the communication of ideas. Gradually, as

skill in controlling materials developed, so did the ability to use the work as a practical means of expression. Wood was patterned and carved, clay pots could be decorated, first with marks and later with coloured clays and glazes. While the crafts continued to be useful, another dimension developed and craftsmen conveyed their own feeling in their work as, for example, in the pottery of China. The craftsman had, in fact, two problems to consider. The first was the functional aspect of his work and the second was the decorative one.

2. We live in a man-made environment surrounded for the most part by man-made objects. It is up to each one of us to select from what is available those things which are the most useful and the ones we like the most. By these means we can help to create our own environment: in the first place by carefully selecting from existing objects and in the second place by actually making things for ourselves: we can make clothes, build furniture, model pots and cook food. As adults we need these sorts of creative opportunities and so do children. The environment is presented to the child in real terms by bringing it within his physical grasp. Education is, for a large part, equipping a child for his adult life, so here we have an opportunity of helping him both as a future designer and as a consumer of goods. We are able to provide some experience by which the creative and critical powers of the child may be developed.

The way we teach pottery in school must be built on these two principles. It seems to me that we can only experiment with materials when the materials have been handled and used: when some skill and understanding of them have been acquired. We need to cover the basic groundwork of technique without neglecting the opportunity for experiment and play as the need arises.

As teachers we have to provide the materials, equipment and advice necessary for the understanding of the craft, together with an environment in which experiments can be made and ideas conceived.

Pottery seems, by this criterion, a suitable activity for three reasons:

1. Clay itself is a material which is immediately responsive. Push it and it changes shape instantly. No tools or equipment are needed and in fact many models and pots can be made using the fingers alone. Yet clay craft can be developed almost to any lengths. Skills can be learned and techniques developed. From simple, direct beginnings, a whole complex craft can be built up.

2. If the pottery room is well managed so that work is not frustrated by bad organization, if the right atmosphere exists for the individual child to work in a group, with each child accepting the responsibility of working logically and systematically through a problem, then we are achieving a real aim—that of equipping a child to accept self responsibility in a group, while working towards an end.

3. The basic equipment necessary for pottery need not daunt the beginner. Initially the minimum of materials is necessary. Clay, either dug by the children or bought from a supplier, is all that is needed in the first place. Sticks, knives, pebbles, string will all serve as useful tools, besides the use of hands alone. Gradually the equipment can be extended as the need arises.

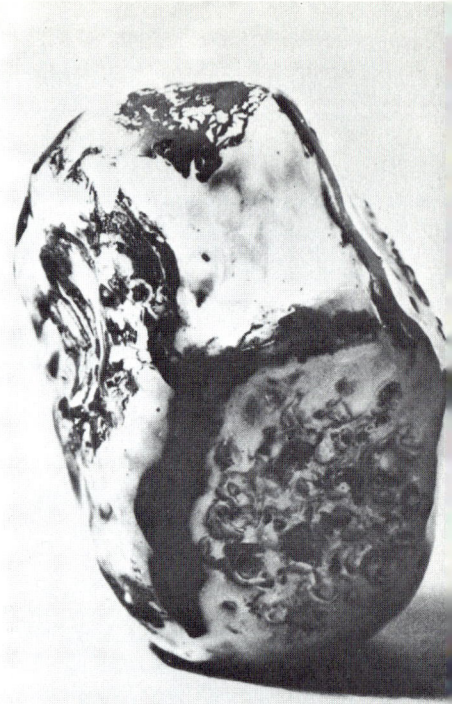

Stones made by joining two thumb pots together, decorated with oxides and opaqu white glaze. Children 14

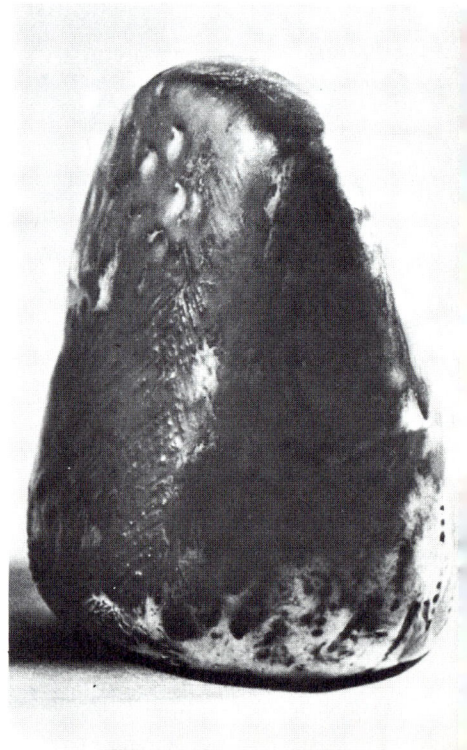

umb pots joined together, using seed forms
a basis for shape. Children 14

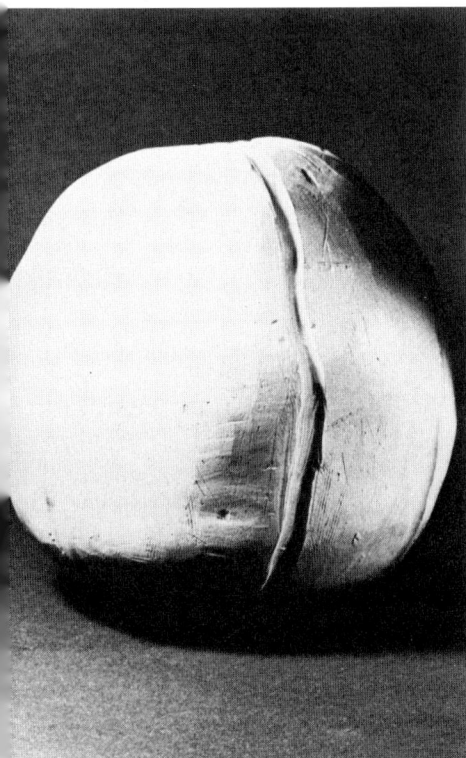

Work in the primary school

Pottery, and in its wider sense, clay work, certainly has its place in the primary school. No syllabus or pattern of work is needed at this stage but some understanding of the underlying principles is essential.

Infant level. A child of five is, for the most part, concerned with exploring his environment. It is now that he needs access to a wide variety of materials—to handle them, play with them and use them. The teacher needs to supply a wide range of materials together with an environment in which these can be used without the feeling that it is in any sense a waste of time. All the materials can be used together—buttons, feathers, cloth, leather, cork and clay can be used by the child all at the same time. Many children will be only too pleased to explore the clay, to mix it with water and some children may try to smear it on their faces. Some children may even find it distasteful and unpleasant and prefer the cleaner feel of sand or bricks.

The child will, in the first place, handle clay, finding out what can and cannot be done. Gradually he will start to use it to give body to that part of his fantasy he finds most important at the time: the fairies, dragons or witches which are as real to him as the things around him.

If a stimulus is required, then the teacher must present a broad idea so that discussion with the children will reveal those things that are most important for them, be it the star of the Nativity or the birthday cake at a party.

Essentially, at this time, the teacher's job is not to direct the children's interest but rather to follow it, providing such materials as are needed with discussion on the child's work while it is in progress. Work need not be fired and any models made have to be kept only for as long as the child shows interest.

Older primary school children. The problem here is more complicated. Craft work may have fallen into two fields of activity. On the one hand will be the use of craft as a means by which knowledge of a practical nature can be explored, such as the knowledge of how to build forts and construct bridges, and how to make historical figures in costume and so on. Here the aim is not to create original work or express ideas, but rather to study what has been made and, in making it, understand it. This work is without doubt useful. But if we restrict the child's craft work to such activities we are depriving him of the chance to express himself.

On the other hand lies the creative work in which the child can express himself and his ideas. We must not, in any sense, judge this work. This will give the impression that there is a right way and a wrong way—which would be fallacious. We ought to provide topics from which ideas can flow; characters from a favourite book, for example, would give a child stimulus and allow him a wide scope for interpretation.

At about nine or ten a child may begin to express dissatisfaction with his own work. 'But it's no good' or 'It's not right' he will say; we have to be prepared to discuss this and offer some solution, either by introducing further skills or by leading the child into another path.

Simple pots can be attempted, though only if they appear to satisfy a need. While some children may find the more serious and technically demanding skill needed for making a thumb or a coil pot requires too much sustained concentration, others will respond with enthusiasm and demand more advanced skills. It is important that children are shown how to do the processes properly and how they relate to each other and form a part of the whole craft. It is a mistake to let children have a try and only half succeed. By this stage the children will begin to take a pride in their finished work and will want it as near perfect as possible.

Thumb pots, coil pots, and simple slab pots can be made together with tiles and slip decoration. More mechanical work, such as making a mould or a mould pot or slip casting, has little or no value as far as creative work goes and should definitely not be attempted.

Unfortunately few primary schools possess or can afford to possess a kiln. If no kiln is available, the work can be kept in its dry raw state and displayed without being fired, with emphasis put on the actual making rather than on the permanence of the finished pot or model. Any work which can be completed and fired, even only to the biscuit stage, will give immense satisfaction.

This, I think, is a good time to have a go at firing in a bonfire. A description of how this can be done is included in the chapter on firing kilns. The results of such firings will be rough and ready, but this is unimportant compared with the satisfaction and pleasure of the experience. Only pots with fairly thin walls should be fired, as there is only a limited amount of control over the heat, and thick walls or models may not stand the strain.

Encourage the children to bring clay from their own gardens or found in the fields, by banks of rivers, from a churchyard, when a grave is being dug, or even a hole in the road. Only a small piece is necessary to show that it has all the qualities of the clay which comes in bags to the school. This will help to relate work in the pottery to the school environment.

Work in the secondary school

In the secondary school crafts are usually separated from the rest of the curriculum and are presented to the pupils as a separate area of activity. By the time children are eleven or twelve, they want a workmanlike approach and want to develop their skills and achieve successful results. It is important to have a basic guide on which individual lessons can be built.

I have made out a guide to the various stages through which pottery has developed through the ages. While I am in no way drawing a parallel between the art produced by Stone Age man and that produced by a child, that art does, nevertheless, introduce the more direct techniques of hand building and modelling; later ages progress through more advanced techniques until work on the potter's wheel is reached.

Any syllabus of work has to be based clearly on three things.
1. The child and his environment.
2. The equipment and limitations of space and time.
3. The personal preferences of the teacher concerned.

So any plan has, of necessity, to be vague; it is up to the teacher to adapt this plan to his own requirements, or to abandon it altogether. The various stages are enumerated for convenience, but each one does not necessarily imply work for any particular length of time.

Simple plant pot kiln
Setting pots in warm ashes before lighting bonfire

Firing bonfire
Sorting out pots from bonfire

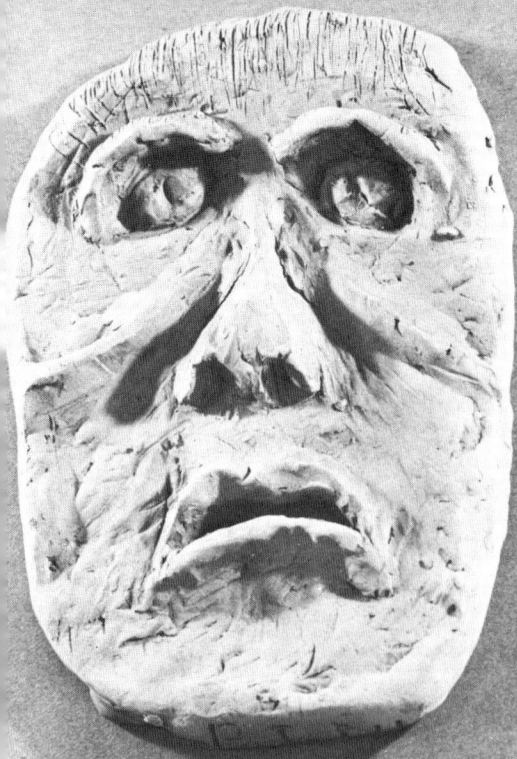

Above: masks on theme of emotion. Children 12

Below: masks with oxide decoration. Children 12

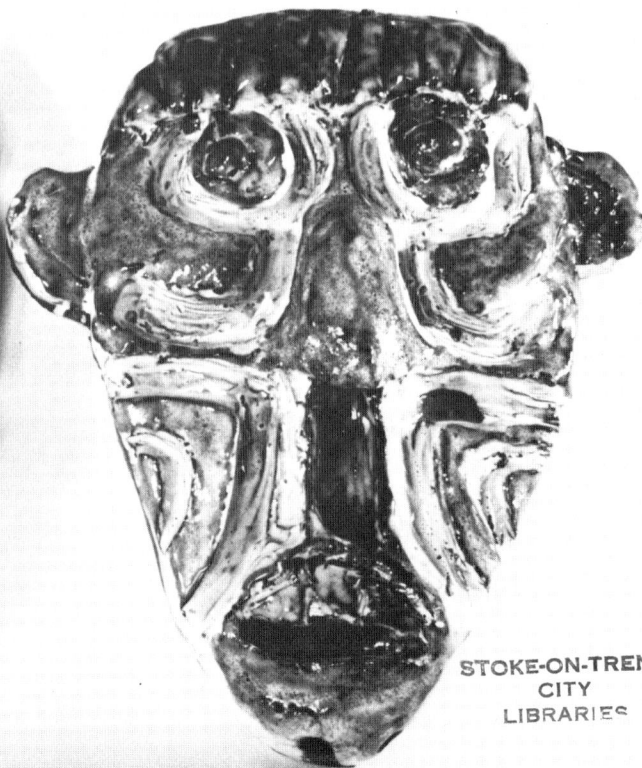

1 Introduction

a. A general acquaintance with clay—collecting, playing, experimenting, preparing it for use.

b. Squeezing from balls of clay forms, such as those that grow under the sea or might grow on another planet.

c. Simple methods of pot building:

   (i) Thumb pots.

   (ii) Pots made from slabs and rolled round square or round objects.

   (iii) Tiles with built-up decoration.

   (iv) Glazes used to complete the process of making a pot rather than as ends in themselves.

   (v) Modelling of any type, but closely related to the children, their interests, environment and fantasy.

2 Experiment

a. More advanced methods of hand-built pottery—coil pots: round, triangular, square.

b. Decoration—its suitability and form.

c. Slipwork—pouring, trailing, feathering.

d. Slab pots and experiments with slabs as units of design, relating together.

e. Simple glaze work.

f. Modelling.

3 Skills

a. Mould pots—conceived as a design and as a method of producing pots suitable for decoration.

b. Colouring oxides and their effect in glazes. Glaze experiments with combinations of simple materials.

c. Throwing on the wheel (simple basic forms).

4 Consolidation

Some grasp of the craft and its use as an art form may be seen by this stage. The ability to see the processes as a whole should be encouraged, though not pursued endlessly. The different methods of pot building need to be correlated as much as possible and experiments of all kinds should be encouraged so that skills can be applied in a personal way, and artificial divisions of technique avoided. Moulded pots, for example, can be joined together to form decorative pots of various sorts; modelling can be carried out on the surface of coil pots. Form, as such, should be considered and work related to plants and buildings, which have a definite and understandable construction.

5 Design

By this stage some understanding of the craft should have developed. Designing and making a pot can be tried. Group projects can be attempted with a view to giving the results a permanent home in the school building. Experiments can be made with sculptural constructions in clay. Problems can be set which deal with the relationship of one area to another, together with the different types of textured surfaces obtainable with clay.

Finally the point is reached at which the relationship between child and teacher is more like that between two craftsmen—one junior and one senior. The child has a real understanding of the organisation involved in pottery, of the careful consideration of the many parts of a problem. Each process is carried out with a craftsman's skill and conscientiousness.

Points of organisation

There are one or two practical points concerning pottery in the classroom which may be of help to teachers who are going to start teaching pottery. Many teachers will already have knowledge and experience of classroom techniques, but these points I have found particularly worth watching:

1 Labelling of work. All work needs to be clearly marked throughout all the stages of its production.

There are several reasons for this:

a. With a large number of children using a classroom it is impossible for a teacher to remember to whom a piece of work belongs.

b. Work left out can quickly be put into the correct place if marked. Pots, while still being made, can be marked with a small piece of paper.

c. After work has dried out or been fired, and shrinkage has taken place, it is often difficult to identify.

d. It is often necessary, when showing or praising work, to know to whom it belongs.

e. It enables finished work to be collected quickly.

f. Pots can be effectively marked on the bottom, and this should be done clearly and neatly. The name can either be scratched on at the leather-hard stage or painted on at the glazing stage with manganese oxide mixed with water.

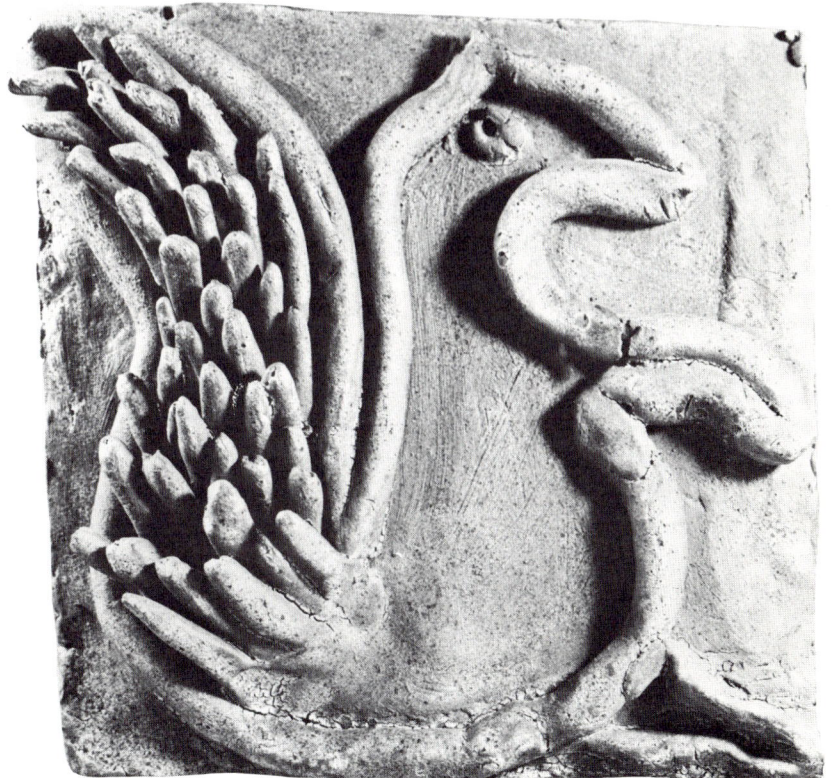

Animal tile. Child 11

2 Lesson arrangement. Again, no rules can be made which will provide the ideal lesson layout, for it depends on the work being done, the number of children and the stage to which they have developed. However, with some straightforward lessons dealing with basic techniques I have found the following arrangement works quite well.

a. *Introduction*. The aim of the lesson should be explained and related to previous work. Pictures or actual pots can form the basic stimulus, but these should be used discreetly and as a complement to the child's own ideas, since once he has seen a particular form, it is often difficult for him to think of a new one, or even a variation of the same one. The method of work can be explained, and any technical points explained. This is also a good time to relate the work to the history of pottery; for example, the making of slipware would be related to the tradition of slipware in England, the making of coil pots to those of, say, Nigeria. If handles are being put on, a selection of photographs showing different types of handles can be shown, and the merits of each discussed.

Clay preparation can precede the demonstration, as this will enable work to be started immediately afterwards. Give each child opportunity to prepare his own clay, but help those who are obviously in difficulties. While it is important to do the whole process, the actual creative work is the most important, and so help may be needed to get over the preliminary stage quickly and efficiently.

b. *Demonstration*. This is important, and needs to be carefully worked out beforehand.

Points to remember:

 (i) Have a clear aim.

 (ii) Demonstrate only one new part at a time.

(iii) Ensure that all necessary equipment is to hand and that the clay is in a suitable working condition.

(iv) Prepare any necessary parts beforehand, e.g. a slab pot needs slabs which have hardened out slightly.

 (v) Keep the demonstration short.

c. *Work*. Having started the group working, let this go on for a time so that a good working atmosphere can be established. Only those children who cannot get started or manage the initial stage will need attention. After a real effort has been made to come to terms with the problem, then individual attention can be given and problems sorted out.

d. *Conclusion*. Most lessons need a conclusion of some sort. This can be some form of group discussion on the work, or a comment from the teacher. Work should not be passed by without some sort of remark, preferably constructive.

Stimulus

Both teacher and pupil need outside stimuli from time to time for a new look or a fresh idea. These may come from photographs of pots, or from seeing the work of established potters; but sometimes a stimulus outside the realm of pottery is needed to encourage individuality and excite the imagination.

On these occasions there are two main sources of inspiration. The first is nature; one can look again at those things which have come about naturally by growth. The second is man-made forms; one can look at the many beautiful and exciting shapes produced by man while working along functional lines.

This new look may involve using a microscope or hand lens, comparing various forms, or even cutting up photographs; but the importance of the stimuli itself should never be lost sight of in the interest of the technique.

1 Natural forms

Seed pods (often a ribbed frame supporting the thinner walls; superb shapes, full, strong and delicate)

Pea and bean pods

Poppyheads, sycamore, acorns, seeds and seed husks of all sorts

Nuts, melons, apples, oranges and citrus fruits in general (full, ripe shapes)

Animals of all sorts, fish, birds (living specimens, also stuffed ones and photographs)

2 Shapes resulting from natural activity

Pebbles, boulders and rocks for shape, colour and texture

Driftwood

Roots

3 Natural or man-made forms providing almost perfect patterns

Natural	*Man-made*
Honeycomb	Tiles on roof
Snowflakes	Willow fences
Shells—sea and land animals	Gothic railway station architecture
Flowers and plants	Manhole covers
Seahorses	
Butterfly wings	

4 Man-made shapes illustrating suitability to function

Stone walls	Iron and steel works
Boats and planes	Blast furnaces
Cooling towers	Gasworks
Lighthouses	Building sites—scaffolding cranes
Windmills	Car engines and component parts
Clocks and watches	Other machines, e.g. bicycles
Bottles	Motor-bicycles
Roofs	Musical instruments

5 Forms and patterns suitable for microscopic examination

a. Plant tissues
   Cross sections of plant stems and roots
   Xylem vessels

b. Animal tissues
   Sections of bones
   Cross sections of animal gut

c. Micro organisms
   Diatoms
   Algae (e.g. spirogyra)
   Foraminiferans

6 Events

(Usually well illustrated with photographs)

International sporting events, international games

Football matches

Pop singers and musical groups

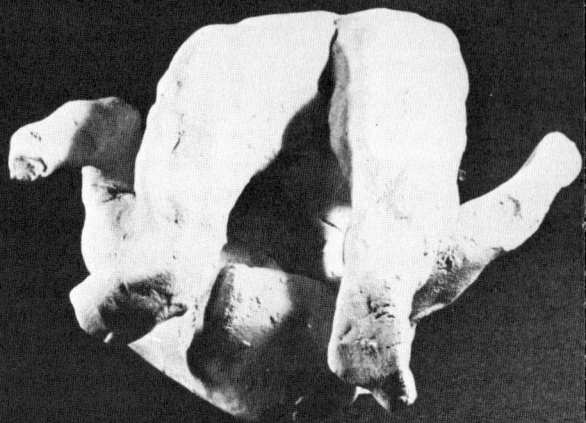

Figures intended to portray movement.
Children 13

Conclusion

For the past 5,000 years or so men have made pots in some form or another. Stone-age man made simple earthenware pots, probably fired in an open fire and used for storing grain. The Ancient Egyptians some 3,000 years ago made beautiful pots and were, perhaps, the first people to discover and use glazes. High temperature firings for stoneware and porcelain were discovered by the Chinese in the eighth century. Clay has the almost miraculous combination of plasticity, which allows it to take on practically any shape, and imperviousness to liquids, when it hardens through the application of heat. As man's skill in handling and controlling clay developed so pottery took on a new dimension. It became decorative as well as functional.

A list of how pottery, in some form or another, is used in modern life is very impressive, ranging from kitchen crockery, bathroom fittings, bricks and tiles to industrial storage jars. Clay is capable of being made into the finest china and porcelain and into extremely tough building materials. It is amazing to think that even today it has a place in the rockets sent to the moon, and in the sparking plugs of engines.

Pottery in school has a useful place. It provides the framework for artistic self-expression and the opportunity for studying the environment in a real way. Work with clay can become more than the mere filling in of time in a 'useful way' or a method by which 'skills' are acquired.

Pottery, along with many other crafts, has a long and varied tradition. As teachers we can refer to past work and draw from it those examples which relate to the present work of the child. So a background is built up. We must not ignore, however, the present flourishing growth of pottery; in recent years there has been an increase in the number of potters producing good, well-designed functional ware. This can be bought, as it is inexpensive, for the school and referred to as necessary. Discussion can decide whether this work is successful functionally and whether or not such work has a value other than its obvious use. Some potters can be visited in their workshops, and various bodies, such as *The Craftsman Potter's Shop* or *The Rural Industries Bureau*, will often provide lists of such craftsmen.

The recent increase in the demand amongst adults for the opportunity to learn and practise crafts has been phenomenal and in many cases met by the local authority's providing a wide range of evening classes. The mass production of goods, essential for social and economic reasons, has seemed to bring about a reaction with some people which takes the form of an increased awareness of design.

By practising the craft of pottery one gains a better understanding of the needs and problems of design and a general awareness of it as part of living. We can hope that this is one of the ways in which a higher standard of design will be achieved and a visually more attractive and lively world created as people become more able to discriminate between good and indifferent work.

If we can enable children to express themselves in visual terms and at the same time foster in them a critical attitude based on an understanding of the problems involved, then we will be achieving a great deal, both for the child of today and the adult of tomorrow.

Appendix 1 : supplies and materials

Materials

Clay

    Plastic, ready for use; packed in $\frac{1}{4}$ or $\frac{1}{2}$ cwt bags

    Red, terra cotta

    White, modelling body (can be purchased later)

Raw Materials

    China clay

    Flint

    Ball clay (can be omitted if other dried clay
        available)

    Whiting (can be added later)

    Feldspar

Ready mixed glazes

    Transparent earthenware glaze

    Opaque White Tin earthenware glaze

Oxides (for colouring)

    Red iron oxide

    Black cobalt oxide (strong and very expensive)

    Copper oxide

    Manganese oxide

    Chrome oxide

    Nickel oxide

    Rutile   } Can be added later.

    Crocus martus   Not essential at first.

    Tin oxide

Frits

    Lead monosilicate

    Lead bisilicate

    Borax frit (i.e. Podmore's 'E')

Equipment

Kiln

Recommended:

a. Cromartie

b. Kilns and Furnaces Ltd

Wheel (added later unless new pottery is being built)
Recommended:

1. Leach type—manufacturers, Woodleys Joinery. Price
   £45 approx.

2. Saviac kick wheel—designed by David Ballantyne—
marketed and manufactured by Wengers. Price £95
approx.
This is a very well designed and efficient wheel. Most
of the parts are adjustable to fit individual
requirements; but it is expensive.

3. Wengers Super 70 Electric Wheel.
Very good: slow even speed; good control: very
expensive—about £100.

Tables   strong and firm, smooth topped

Sieve   80 mesh to start, then add 60 and 100

Buckets   for glaze and slip

Bins   for clay

Damp cupboard or *biscuit tins*

Sheets of polythene — (clay from the suppliers is usually
wrapped in good sized sheets which can be kept and
used.)

Tiles or *asbestos batts*

Wires for cutting clay

Brushes: glaze mops
               liners and shaders

Sponges: small, natural; synthetic

Rolling pins

Rolling guides

Bowls — large and small

Pestle and mortar (not essential)

Slip trailers

Suppliers

Thomas E. Gray and Co Ltd
37 Headlands, Kettering
all clays, grogs and some raw materials

Cromartie Kilns Ltd
Park Hall Road, Longton, Staffordshire
electric kilns

Judson and Hudson Ltd
Keighley, Yorkshire
electric wheels

Kilns and Furnaces Ltd
Keele Street Works, Tunstall, Stoke-on-Trent

Podmore and Sons Ltd
Stoke-on-Trent
general supplies, raw materials

Wengers Ltd
Stoke-on-Trent
kilns, wheels, sundries

Technical Art Products
202 Turnpike Link, East Croydon, Surrey
brush wax; liquid wax resist

Saviac Workshop
2 Chewton Farm Road, Highcliff, Hampshire
Plans for electric, oil or gas kilns and other equipment

Woodleys Joinery Works
Newton Poppleford, Devon
Leach kick wheel

Appendix 2 : recipes

Slip recipes

1. White
Ball clay 90%
Red clay 10%
Coloured slips are made by adding oxides to this base.

2. Green
2–5 per cent copper
0·5 per cent cobalt will soften it slightly

3. Blue
0·5–2 per cent cobalt
   1 per cent copper

4. Tan (no oxides necessary)
Ball clay 50%
Red clay 50%

5. Black (base red clay)
Iron oxide 7%
Manganese oxide 5%
Cobalt oxide 2%

Glaze recipes

These recipes have proved fairly reliable over a period of time but are essentially a guide and may need adjusting slightly to suit individual requirements and clay bodies. All mature around 1080°C. Cone 01a

Transparent glazes

1. Lead bisilicate 70
  China clay 26
  Flint 4
2. Lead monosilicate 60
  Feldspar 18
  Whiting 6
  Flint 8
  China clay 8

Basic transparent glaze + additions (for coloured results)

Opaque grey green
Tin oxide 8%
Copper oxide 6%
Nickel oxide 3%
Cobalt oxide 1%

Speckled grey
Tin oxide 8%
Copper carbonate 5%
Manganese oxide 2%

Transparent green grey
Copper oxide 5%
Cobalt 0·5%
Iron 0·5%

Pale transparent green
Copper oxide 5%
Iron oxide 0·5%

Soft evening blue
Copper oxide 3%
Cobalt oxide 1%
Manganese oxide 2%
+8% Tin oxide for opaque glaze

Bright blue
Cobalt oxide 2%
Zinc oxide 2%

Black
Copper oxide 3%
Manganese oxide 2%
Iron oxide 5%
Cobalt oxide 1%

Any transparent glaze can be made opaque by the addition of 10 per cent tin oxide.

Black glaze (matt)

Lead monosilicate 70%
China clay 19%
Alumina oxide 3%
Tin oxide 8%
Manganese oxide 2%
Iron oxide 2%
Cobalt oxide 0·5%

Alkaline glaze

Alkaline frit 55
Feldspar 30
Whiting 6
China clay 4
Quartz 5
Copper oxide 1

Broken white

Calcined borax 24
Feldspar 30
Whiting 10
Clay 20
Flint 16

Glossary

Biscuit firing   The first firing to which pottery is subjected.

Body   The various clays used for making pots are generally known as the body.

China clay   Pure primary clay; the English name for Kaolin (Chinese) which means in Chinese 'high ridge', from the place where the clay is found.

Chuck   A lump of clay placed on the wheelhead for supporting pots.

Clay   A plastic malleable earth occurring naturally over the earth's surface, the result of the decomposition of feldspathic rock.

Coil pots   Method of pot building using coils or rings of clay joined together.

Cones   Temperature indicators used in kilns, made from glaze materials, in the shape of pyramids.

Encaustic tiles   Were made in England during the Middle Ages. Clay was inlaid in a tile of contrasting colour; consequently the pattern was not lost as the tile began to wear down.

Feathering   A method of decoration whereby two slips of different colour are laid next to each other and a bristle is pulled across to run one into the other.

Feldspar   Igneous rock which when decomposed gives clay. Has all the ingredients of clay plus other salts and fluxes which make it an ideal glaze material. Melts at 1250°C.

Fettling   Preparing pots for the kiln; removing glaze on feet, checking for chipped glaze.

Flux   An essential glaze ingredient which causes the other ingredients to fuse.

Frit   A manufactured glaze material: two or more raw materials are heated until they melt, poured into cold water, which shatters the glass, and ground to powder. Frits are necessary when either poisonous or soluble materials are being used.

Glaze   Glassy surface on pots: serves both a decorative and functional purpose.

Grog   Powdered, fired clay. Often added to clay to reduce shrinkage and open the body.

Impervious   Cannot be penetrated by water or liquids.

Incised decoration   Decoration pressed or cut into the surface of the clay.

Kneading   A method of clay preparation similar to wedging, except that the movements are more peaceful and rhythmic; best for removing air bubbles and moving the molecules evenly.

Layering   Cutting a block of clay into slabs with a nylon or copper wire.

Luting   The joining together of clay parts while leather-hard.

Muffle   A wall of firebricks which protects pots from the flames in a flame-burning kiln.

Opacifier   A substance, usually a metal oxide which, when added to a transparent glaze, suspends itself in the glaze to render it opaque and white.

Oxides   Metal oxides produced industrially used for colouring clays and glazes.

Plaster of Paris   Powdered and heated gypsum which sets hard when mixed with water.

Porcelain   Very fine pottery body made by mixing china clay and china stone. A high temperature is required to give the resulting translucency.

Pyrometer   An instrument used for registering the temperature inside a kiln.

Reclaim   Clay which has been used but not fired, softened down in water and put out to harden for re-use.

Refractory   With the capacity to withstand great heat.

Saggar   Boxes made out of fireclay and grog in which pots are packed in the kiln to protect them from the flames.

Seal   The mark made by potters on the pot to identify the maker.

Sgraffito   The Italian word meaning 'scratched'. A decorative method whereby the surface is scratched to reveal a different colour, i.e. through a layer of slip or glaze.

Slab pots   Pots built by using flat pieces of clay. These can either be bent into moulds or used flat in a sort of ceramic carpentry.

Slip   Clay softened down in water, put through a 60 or 80 mesh sieve until it has the consistency of cream. It can be coloured by the addition of oxides and used for decoration.

Slurry   Clay softened down in water to a messy uneven and formless mass.

Sprigging	The method of decoration used extensively by Wedgwood to produce his Jasper ware. A fine mould is used to produce the sprig which is then applied to the surface of the pot.
Spurs	Three-cornered supports made in a fine white body used for supporting pots, glazed on the bottom, in an earthenware firing.
Throwing	The art of building up pots on a potter's wheel using centrifugal force.
Thumb pots	Simple pots made by squeezing clay between the thumb and fingers, sometimes called pinch pots.

Turning	Removing surplus clay from a thrown pot —rather like wood-turning on a lathe.
Vitrified	Like glass, fused together.
Wedging	The systematic preparation of clay before starting work. It has three functions:

1. Makes the clay homogeneous by breaking down hard lumps.
2. Removes air bubbles.
3. Tends to make the clay stronger by moving the molecules in approximately the same direction.

Bibliography and reference sources

Leach, Bernard *A Potter's Book* Faber 1945
Excellent reading both for providing a background to the studio pottery movement in this country and for numerous facts and points of reference.
Green, D. *Pottery Materials & Techniques* Faber 1967
Well presented and organized material. Very useful for reference of all techniques.
Green, D. *Understanding Pottery Glazes* Faber 1963
For detailed knowledge of raw materials and their effect in glazes, glaze calculations and tables of reference.
Billington, Dora M. *The Technique of Pottery* Batsford 1962
A reference book which covers all studio techniques.
Röttger, Ernst *Creative Clay Craft* Batsford 1963
Well illustrated work of children and students. Very good for stimulus and ideas.
Kenny, J. B. *Complete Book of Pottery Making* Greenberg New York 1949
Excellent for processes and glaze recipes.
Rhodes Daniel *Kilns: Design, Construction and Operation* Pitman 1969
An informative, well illustrated history of kiln design, with advice on the construction of many types of kilns.
Cardew, M. *Pioneer Pottery* Longman 1969
Deals with advanced pottery techniques.
Lewis, Griselda *Picture History of English Pottery* Hulton 1956
A fascinating background to English pottery from the Bronze Age to the present day.
Haggar, R. G. *Pottery Through the Ages* Methuen 1959
An outline survey of pottery from the beginning to the present (industrial) scene.

The Faber Monographs on Pottery and Porcelain
Each book has a brief text with plenty of illustrations and deals with one aspect of pottery of the past.
Pottery Quarterly
Northfields Studio, Northfields, Tring, Hertfordshire.
Year's subscription £1 6s 0d
Ideal for view of contemporary work.
Craftsman Potter's Shop of Great Britain
William Blake House, Marshall Street, London W1.
A shop selling work by some of the best contemporary potters. Associate membership will ensure a bi-monthly newsletter plus advance knowledge of all meetings and lectures arranged by the organization. A limited range of potters' sundries is sold.
The Craft Centre of Great Britain
43 Earlham Street, London WC1.
All crafts represented and excellent work on view.

Slides and photographs of pots, for hire or sale
Slide Loans (Ceramics) and Films
Fournier Pottery: Castle Hill Cottages, Brenchley, Tonbridge, Kent.
Pictorial Colour Slides: 242 Langley Way, West Wickham, Kent
Filmstrips
Diana Wyllie Ltd: 3 Park Road, London NW1.
Common Ground Ltd: 44 Fulham Road, London SW3.
(*Potter* Raymond Finch; filmstrips and notes)
Brun Educational Films Ltd: 15 Prestwich Street, Burnley.
(Film loops on pottery technique)

London Art
Bishop
351